D0986236

MODES
for Guitar

by TOM KOLB

ISBN 978-0-634-01877-0

HAL•LEONARD®
CORPORATION

7777 W. BLUEMOUND RD. P.O. BOX 13819 MILWAUKEE, WI 53213

Visit Hal Leonard Online at
www.halleonard.com

About the Author

Tom Kolb has been an instructor at Musicians Institute (G.I.T.) since graduating with vocational honors and the "Student of the Year" award in 1989. He teaches such core curriculum classes as Single-String Improvisation, Rhythm Guitar, and Rhythm Section Workshop, as well as popular electives like Melodic Soloing and Classic Rock Live Playing Workshop. Tom is Associate Editor and featured columnist for *Guitar One* magazine, and is the featured artist on over a dozen Star Licks and Hal Leonard instructional videos.

A veteran of over 4,000 gigs, Tom has toured the U.S. and Europe, serving as a sideman and/or musical director for major artists as well as playing with his own band, the Gurus. Currently maintaining a busy schedule of live dates and recording sessions, he enjoys juggling his playing/teaching/songwriting career in the Los Angeles area.

Acknowledgments

I would like to thank my wife Hedy and daughter Flynnie for their unconditional love and support; my mom and dad for encouraging me in my music career; everyone at Hal Leonard Corporation, *Guitar One*, and Star Licks; Musicians Institute; and last but not least, my students, without whom I would probably lack the perennial drive to keep growing as a musician.

CD Production Credits

Guitars, bass, and keyboards: Tom Kolb
Engineering and drum programming: Dale Turner
Recorded at Intimate Audio

Contents

Introduction

The modes of the major scale have long been a fascinating subject for guitarists. But at the same time, they can be a great source of confusion and misunderstanding. The purpose of this book is to unravel the mysteries of the modes and to guide you through the world of their applications. We'll take an in-depth look at how modes can be used in various soloing situations, as a source for creating riffs, and as tools for writing unique chord progressions.

Each chapter contains suggested fretboard patterns, licks, and musical examples, as well as valuable insights into each mode's unique application. Each example is demonstrated on the accompanying CD. There is also a jam track featuring a "play-along progression" for each mode, so you can practice applying the modes in an improvisational setting. As a special bonus, in the final chapter, we'll explore some of the modes of other popular scales.

Although it's highly recommended that you start at the beginning of this book and work your way through to the end, if you prefer, you can jump in anywhere, especially if you're already familiar with a mode or two. You can always refer back to the first chapter, "Theory of the Modes," if you find yourself getting confused.

Dig in and have fun!

—Tom Kolb

About the Recording

Every musical example in this book is demonstrated on the accompanying CD. Tracks with a full rhythm section are played twice—once at normal speed and then again at half speed. For the normal-speed examples, the featured guitar is mixed hard right. This allows you to play along either with the entire mix, or, by adjusting the balance to the left, with just the rhythm section.

Don't forget—there's a jam track for each mode, so you can practice applying what you've just learned in an improvisational setting. You can work on soloing all over the neck with the various finger patterns provided, experiment with the musical examples presented in the text, and apply the concepts presented in the "Odds and Ends" section at the end of each chapter.

Use Track ◆**1**◆ of the CD to tune your guitar.

The Theory of the Modes

What Are Modes?

Modes are simply scales, or more precisely, "scales within scales." They are created by shifting the tonal center away from the root—or tonic—of a scale, to another note of that same scale, thereby creating a new tonality. For example, when you play the C major scale from its root (C) to its octave, it has the familiar "do-re-mi..." major scale sound due to the order of intervals, or intervallic formula: whole–whole–half–whole–whole–whole–half.

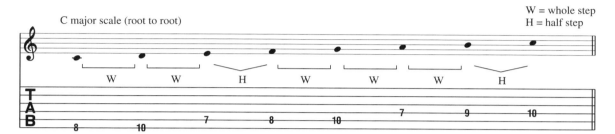

Now, if you play the C major scale again but start on the second note (D) and play up to its octave, you are playing a "mode" of the C major scale. You should notice that it doesn't sound like C major at all, even though you're playing the same notes. This is because you've "shifted" the order of the intervals by starting on the second note. Now the intervallic formula is: whole–half–whole–whole–whole–half–whole. Thus, a "scale within a scale."

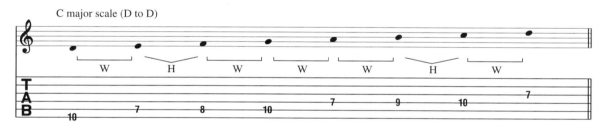

This process can be applied to the other notes of the C major scale as well. And since the C major scale has seven notes (C–D–E–F–G–A–B), it contains seven modes.

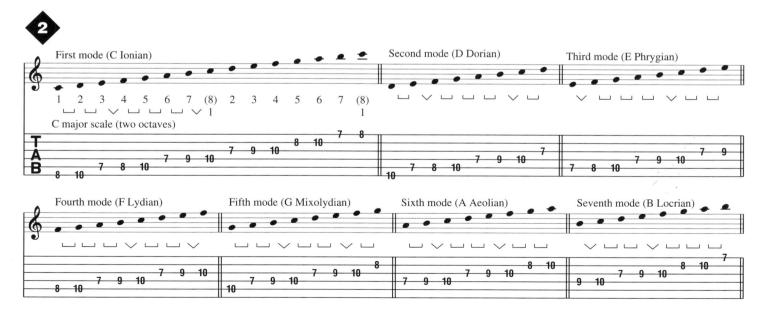

The Names of the Modes

The unusual names of the major scale modes are derived from the Greek language. You'll want to memorize them—and their order—as quickly as possible:

1. **Ionian** (modal name for the major scale, pronounced "eye-own-ee-un")
2. **Dorian** (pronounced "door-ee-un")
3. **Phrygian** (pronounced "fridge-ee-un")
4. **Lydian** (pronounced "lid-ee-un")
5. **Mixolydian** (pronounced "mix-oh-lid-ee-un")
6. **Aeolian** (modal name for the natural minor scale, pronounced "ay-oh-lee-un")
7. **Locrian** (pronounced "low-kree-un")

Even though they may contain various sharps or flats, *all* major scales share the same intervallic formula. Therefore, the process for constructing the seven modes of each is exactly the same as illustrated in the key of C. So, for example, if you were to play an E major scale (E–F♯–G♯–A–B–C♯–D♯) starting from the second degree (F♯), you would be playing F♯ Dorian (second mode). Likewise, if you were to start on the fifth degree (B) of E major, you would be playing B Mixolydian (fifth mode).

NOTE: Any diatonic, seven-note, scale contains within it seven modes (see the "Other Modes" chapter for examples). But for purposes of clarity, this chapter will focus on the modes of the major scale—by far, the most common.

The Parent Scale

A term that will be used throughout this book is *parent scale*. Simply put, this refers to the major scale that a mode is derived from. For example, C major is the parent scale of D Dorian. C major is also the parent scale of E Phrygian, F Lydian, G Mixolydian, and so on. The importance of knowing the parent scale of a mode will become clear as you work your way through this book. For now, here is a three-step, fill-in-the-blanks process that will help you to name the parent scale of any mode:

Example

To find the parent scale of A Lydian:
Step 1) Lydian is the fourth mode.
Step 2) A is the fourth scale step of E major.
Step 3) E major is the parent scale of A Lydian.

Using this process, spend some time drilling yourself to find the parent scales to all of the modes, in as many keys as possible. Here's a blank form to help you get started.

To find the parent scale of __ _____:
Step 1) _____ is the _____ mode.
Step 2) __is the _____ scale step of __ major.
Step 3) __ major is the parent scale of __ _____.

Needless to say, your knowledge of major scales and their key signatures will determine how rapidly you will find the answers. (NOTE: The music notation in this book uses the key signature of the parent scale to represent each mode.)

How Modes Are Used

Now that you know what modes are and where they come from, the question is, "How are they used?" From a "big picture" point of view, the answer is threefold:

1. As melodic devices for soloing over diatonic chord progressions in major and minor keys.
2. As melodic devices for soloing over "modal" progressions.
3. As a source for creating "altered" scales.

1. Modes and Diatonic Progressions

To understand how modes are used in diatonic chord progressions, it's necessary to have a basic knowledge of major scale harmony (refer to the "Aeolian" chapter for a discussion on minor scale harmony). The notes of the C major scale can be harmonized (stacked in thirds) to build a diatonic triad or seventh chord from each scale degree:

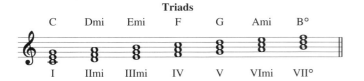

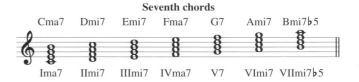

These chords constitute the harmonic palette for the key of C major—the range of possible harmonies you'll find in a diatonic progression. Each chord has a *quality* (major, minor, etc.) and a *function* (I, II, III, IV, etc.) determined by its position within the scale. Although the triads omit the seventh degree, the basic chord qualities and functions remain the same. This results in a chord order formula that applies to all major keys—and memorizing the above Roman numeral formula(s) makes it possible to analyze any major key progression.

Here are some "guitar-friendly" voicings of the seventh chords from above. Play them in order up and down the neck, and you should hear the underlying sound of the major scale.

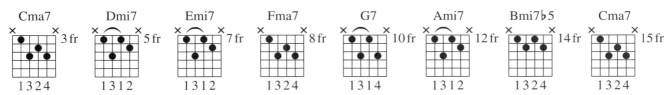

Just as there is a designated chord for each scale step, there is a corresponding mode for each chord. For example, over the II chord (Dmi or Dmi7) in a C major progression, the ear wants to "hear" the corresponding mode—D Dorian—because it's the diatonic choice (Dmi7 is the II chord in C, and D Dorian is the second mode of C). Likewise, if the V chord (G7) comes along, the fifth mode (G Mixolydian) is the "proper" choice.

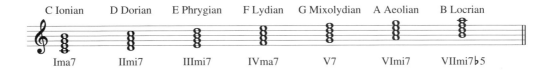

For a quick and easy, hands-on demonstration of how this concept works (without having to learn a boatload of patterns), have a friend play the chords, or listen to the accompanying CD, while you play the following musical exercise:

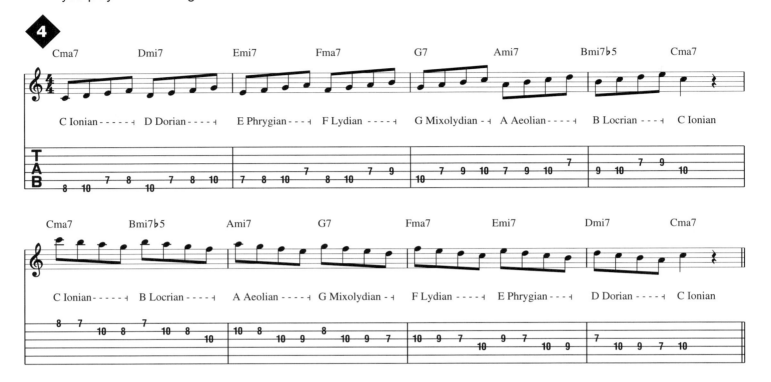

Staying strictly to one pattern of the C major scale, this popular "groups-of-four" sequence nails the first four scale degrees of each mode in the first four measures, while the last four measures involve the top half of each mode played in a descending fashion. Every note of each mode is accounted for in this streamlined exercise. Play the example again and listen to how each set of notes outlines the harmony. But keep in mind that this exercise is mainly for demonstration purposes. In reality, this "modal" approach works best when a chord lasts long enough (one or more measures) for a melody to be fully developed. Incidentally, some refer to this method as treating each change like a temporary "I" ("one") chord.

2. Modes and Modal Progressions

We've seen how the major scale can be harmonized to create chords built from each scale degree. The same process can be applied to the modes to create "modal harmony." And when the chords from a specific mode are used to create a chord progression, it is called a "modal progression." (This will be discussed in greater detail in each of the following chapters.) As an example, if you were to harmonize D Dorian in seventh chords, the order of chords would be Dmi7–Emi7–Fma7–G7–Ami7–Bmi7b5–Cma7.

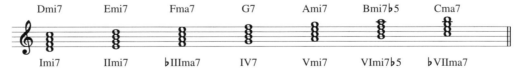

Yes, these chords all belong to the key of C major—the parent scale of D Dorian—but here, Dmi7 is the tonic, or I chord, so each chord now serves a different function (reflected by the Roman numeral analysis).

Now, if you were to build a progression around the Dmi7 chord (I chord) using some or all of the other chords in this harmonized mode, you would be creating a modal progression—in this case, a D Dorian progression. In other words, D Dorian is the key center, and the D Dorian mode is the ideal choice for improvising.

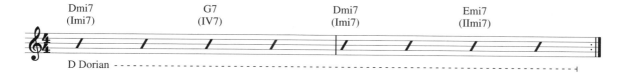

3. Modes as "Altered" Scales

Theoretically, there are specific modes that the ear "wants" or "expects" to hear in a diatonic progression. But sometimes the element of surprise is desired while improvising, and it often surfaces in the form of dissonance, or tension. The superimposing of modes and the mixing-and-matching of *parallel modes* (different modes sharing the same root) can be handy improvisational tools for achieving this type of effect. For instance, A Phrygian might be used where A Aeolian is the more likely candidate; F Lydian could take the place of F Ionian; G Mixolydian and G Dorian might be juggled back and forth over a G7 chord for a delightfully bluesy outcome; etc. The list is endless, but the results are all the same—dissonance, tension, alteration. (All of these concepts will be discussed in depth in later chapters.)

This style of playing is particularly effective when a chord lasts for two or more measures, allowing the player time to develop more complexities in the melody. In order for this modal style of playing to work, you need to follow some type of system, or the results will be chaotic. What many players do is group the modes into specific categories. Here is a simple system that places all of the modes into two basic categories:

Major Modes	Minor Modes
Ionian	Dorian
Lydian	Phrygian
Mixolydian	Aeolian
	Locrian

The modes in the left-hand column all contain a major 3rd degree and can be used over major-type chords. The modes on the right have a minor 3rd and are for minor chords. Of course, this is oversimplification—there are many more factors involved. But this gives the player a "ground zero," fairly consonant starting point from which to launch extended, altered, and even highly dissonant melodies.

Remember this: Once you know the rules well, *then* you'll be able to break them with authority.

Ionian

*QUICK REFERENCE GUIDE

Formula:	1–2–3–4–5–6–7
Construction:	W–W–H–W–W–W–H
Category:	Major
Differentiating scale degree:	7
For chord types:	major, ma6, ma6/9, ma7, ma9, ma13, ma13add4
Harmony:	Ima7–IImi7–IIImi7–IVma7–V7–VImi7–VIImi7♭5
Common progressions:	I–IV–V; IImi–V–I; I–VImi–IV–V; I–IIImi–IV–I; I–IV–I; I–V–I
Five patterns:	C Ionian
	(circled notes are the roots; notes in parentheses are the 7th degrees)

Pattern 1	Pattern 2	Pattern 3	Pattern 4	Pattern 5
	2fr	5fr	7fr	8fr

The Ionian mode outlines the basic structure of a major seventh chord: root, 3rd, 5th, and 7th; and these extensions: 9th, 11th, and 13th.

*NOTE: This *Quick Reference Guide* appears below each chapter heading of the seven modes. *Formula* represents the scale steps of the mode, relative to the major scale. *Construction* pertains to the order of whole- and half-step intervals. *Category* designates whether the mode is major or minor in tonality (containing a major 3rd or minor 3rd scale degree). *Differentiating scale degree* points out which note sets that mode apart from others in its category. *For chord types* lists several chord types for which the mode is commonly used. *Harmony* lists the chord qualities (in seventh chords) when the mode is harmonized. *Common progressions* offers a short list of popular progressions harmonized from the mode. *Five patterns* features five suggested patterns of the mode (using the Musicians Institute numbering system) as they lie in order along the fretboard.

The "Fundamental" Major Mode

Ionian is the modal name for the major scale. Not only is it the fundamental mode, it is the fundamental scale in music, and the scale by which all others are compared. The melodies and harmonies of the Ionian mode are ubiquitous and thoroughly ingrained on our musical psyche, having been a part of our lives since infancy when we first heard them in nursery rhymes. But for all of its familiarity, for some strange reason the Ionian mode is often difficult for guitarists to use in soloing. The "awkward" half-step intervals between the 3rd and 4th degrees, and the 7th and the root, are often at the heart of the problem. That's why many players rely heavily on the major pentatonic scale to solo over major chords and keys. It omits those half-step intervals by leaving out the 4th and the 7th degrees of the scale (key of C: C–D–E–G–A). Nevertheless, while the major pentatonic scale does have plenty to offer, it doesn't include the suspended sound of the 4th and the "leading-tone" pull of the 7th degree, two essential components of the Ionian mode.

Ionian Licks and the Five-Pattern System

The following five figures are all one-bar C Ionian licks. Designed to get you acquainted with MI's "five-pattern system," they also feature an array of half-step moves—7th to the root, 3rd to the 4th scale degrees, and vice versa.

Fig. 1 is a simple melodic statement in C Ionian pattern 1. (NOTE: Pattern 1, of any scale, is based around the open-position C chord voicing. And just as an open-position chord can be transposed by transforming it to barre-chord form, the pattern is also "movable" to any key.) Starting on the root, it drops to the 7th degree, rises to the 5th and resolves to the "melodic" major 3rd. Although it omits the 2nd and 6th degrees of the mode, it is distinctively Ionian by nature due to the emphasis on the 3rd and inclusion of the 7th and 4th degrees. Memorize this lick, and play it in other octaves on different positions of the neck. Then transpose it to other keys.

Fig. 2 is a classically influenced, pedal-point figure in C Ionian pattern 2. (Pattern 2 is based on the barre-chord form of an open-position A chord voicing.) Not only is the root (C) the pedal point, it is clearly the "pitch axis" upon which the entire melody revolves, thus providing the undeniable Ionian flavor.

Half-step bends are the catalysts for getting at the juicy notes in the bluesy C Ionian lick in **Fig. 3**. Using the upper half of pattern 3 (based on the barre-chord form of an open-position G chord voicing), the bend/release moves demonstrate how to rub some of the "sweetness" out of the "too-pretty" effect the 7th and 4th degrees of Ionian can sometimes create.

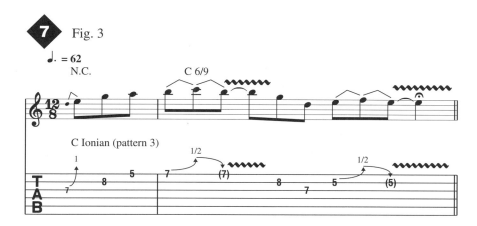

The orchestral C Ionian lick in **Fig. 4** climbs pattern 4 (based on the barre-chord form of an open-position E chord voicing) in a "switchback" sequence of hammer-ons and pull-offs. Notice that each resolving hammer or pull results in a chord tone of Cma13.

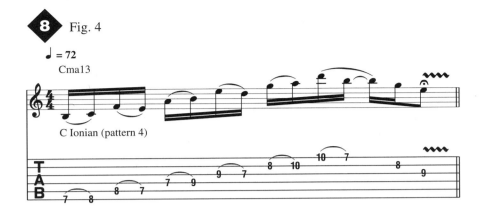

The speedy C Ionian lick in **Fig. 5** scoots down the upper regions of pattern 5 (an extended three-notes-per-string pattern loosely based on the barre-chord form of an open-position D chord voicing), where it then leaps back-and-forth over a few wide intervals and resolves to the root on the sixth string.

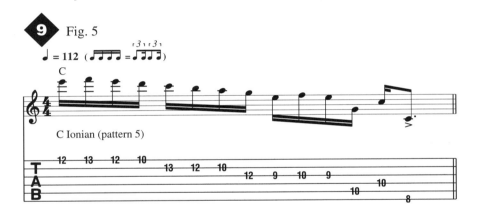

Using Ionian in Key Center Playing

We've seen how the Ionian mode can be used over solitary major chords, and how the 7th and 4th scale degrees help to bring out the distinctive "sound" of the mode. Now let's take a look at how those notes come into play in a major-key chord progression.

Fig. 6 is a I–V–VImi–I–IIImi–IV triad progression in the key of E major, making it an excellent vehicle for the E Ionian mode. The transcribed solo takes a simple yet effective approach toward the use of the mode. Stripping things down to a "guitar-friendly" E major pentatonic framework, it holds off including the omitted notes (4th and 7th) until the arrival of certain chords. The 7th (D♯) makes its first appearance on the V chord (B) and then again on the IIImi (G♯mi) change. The 4th degree is thrown into the mix at the last second on the A (IV) chord. Notice that all of these note choices are strong component notes of the chords being played at the time.

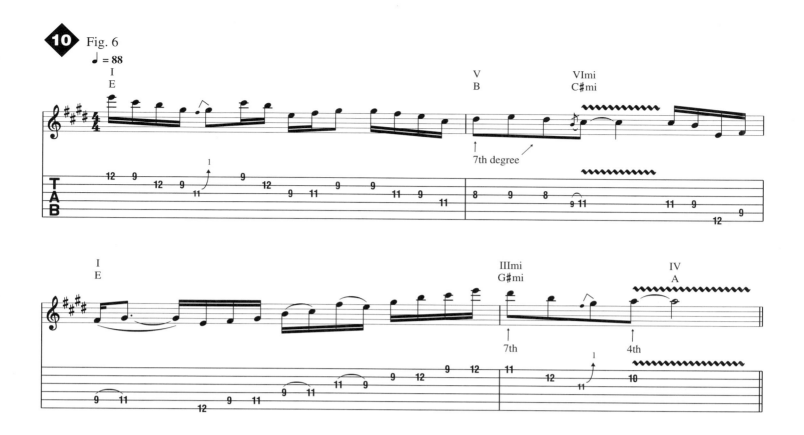

Fig. 7 uses the same approach over a bluesy II–V–I in F major. The line exploits the F major pentatonic scale for the most part but hits the 7th degree (E) of F Ionian on the downbeat of the V chord (C7), nailing the change.

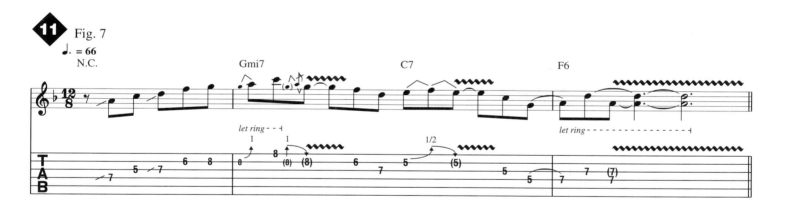

The above examples illustrate the potential of the *differentiating note* of Ionian (the 7th degree—or leading tone) and its impact when used strategically. The secret to using it successfully lies in knowing which chords contain that note in their basic makeup. Upon analysis, you'll find that the IIImi, V, and VII° chords all contain the 7th, or leading tone. You'd be hard pressed to find many VII° or VIImi7♭5 chords in major progressions, but there certainly is an abundance of V and IIImi chords. So when you come across them, don't forget to deploy the "secret weapon"—the 7th degree of Ionian. And don't overlook the resourcefulness of the 4th degree either; use it over IImi and IV chords.

More Ionian Phrases

The legato lick in **Fig. 8** pairs two arpeggios (C and Emi7) harmonized from the C Ionian mode for a decidedly Cma9 outcome.

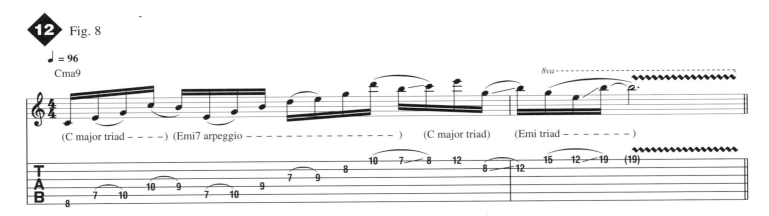

The Eric Johnson -inspired D Ionian pedal-tone lick in **Fig. 9** features some fancy string-skipping moves and a couple of cool half-step slides.

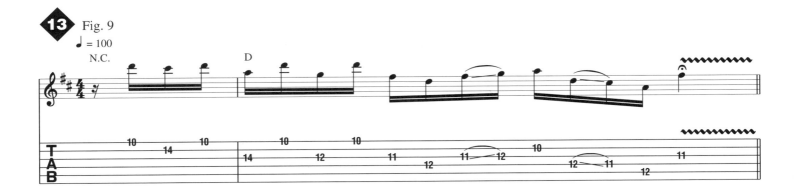

Fig. 10 offers an example of the "fiery" Ionian sensibilities of melodic rock masters such as Tom Scholz (Boston) and Neal Schon (Journey). Constructed from patterns 1 and 2 of G Ionian, the phrase jumbles a multitude of interesting rhythms. Notice though that the sustained notes are all strategically placed, always on a strong chord tone of each new change.

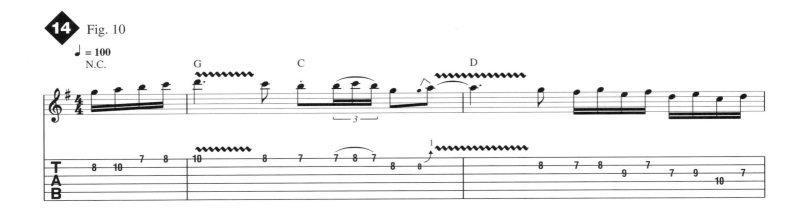

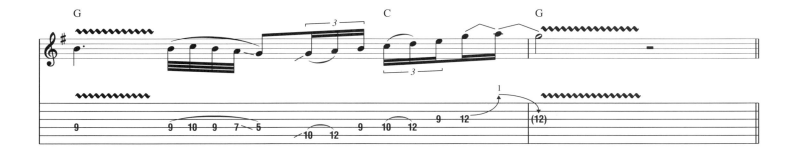

Odds and Ends

Here's a list of additional tips for creating your own C Ionian licks. When you have them down, transpose them to other keys. Be aware that when applying them, you need to establish the root of Ionian as the pitch axis.

1. Play C and G major pentatonic licks. Combined, they represent every note of C Ionian (NOTE: C Ionian can also be viewed as A and E minor pentatonic scales combined).
2. Combine the I, IV, and V major triads (C, F, and G).
3. Borrow licks from the relative minor scale (A minor), maintaining "C" as the pitch axis.
4. Play a Cma7 arpeggio and add the 4th (F).

Play-Along Progression

Use the five patterns of Ionian, located at the top of this chapter, to jam over this C Ionian progression. You can use any of the tips in the "Odds and Ends" section as they are all in C Ionian. Also, try to apply some of the licks in this chapter, changing the rhythms and transposing them where necessary.

Dorian

The "Kinder, Gentler" Minor Mode

Dorian is the second mode of the major scale. (A Dorian is constructed by starting from the second note of the G major scale: A–B–C–D–E–F♯–G.) It is a *minor* mode—that is to say, it is more closely related to the natural minor scale (or Aeolian, its modal name) than it is to the major scale. If you compare the two (Aeolian: 1–2–♭3–4–5–♭6–♭7; Dorian: 1–2–♭3–4–5–6–♭7), you'll find that the only difference is that Dorian has a raised—or "natural"—6th degree. The natural 6th gives Dorian a "lighter" or "softer" sound than the dramatic, often "heavy" sounding Aeolian mode. The Dorian mode can be heard extensively in jazz, blues, and rock music, and is featured prominently in the blues-rock solos of guitarists such as Jimi Hendrix, Carlos Santana, Stevie Ray Vaughan, Jimmy Page, and Robby Krieger.

To get the sound of Dorian in your ears, go through the five patterns of A Dorian just as you would with any scale—running them up and down, playing sequences, etc. Some or all of the patterns may feel "familiar" to your fingers as being patterns of G major. This of course makes sense, as G is the parent scale of A Dorian, but be aware that the tonic—or root note—in these patterns is A. Make a habit of starting and stopping on the root until you have the Dorian sound in your head. Pay strict attention to where the 6th degree (F♯) is located in each of the patterns, as it is the differentiating note of Dorian—the note that distinguishes it from the other minor modes.

Dorian Licks

Now that you have the A Dorian patterns under your fingers, it's time to create some licks. A great place to start is by giving pattern 4 a bit of a facelift. If you remove the 2nd (B) and 6th (F♯) degrees of the pattern, you'll find that the A minor pentatonic scale lies beneath it.

A minor pentatonic

Reversing this process reveals that the Dorian mode can be considered the minor pentatonic scale with an added 2nd (9th) and 6th. Indeed, many fine players (especially in rock and blues) tend to use it this way. This system allows you to use all of your "tried-and-true" minor-pentatonic phrases while only having to "shift" your thinking process a little—by locating and including the missing 9th and 6th degrees. **Fig. 1** offers an example of this process, staying within the confines of A Dorian, pattern 4 .

Fig. 2 is an easy-going A Dorian lick in pattern 2. Notice that it begins with an Ami9 arpeggio (A–B–C–E–G). This is a good string of notes (1–2–♭3–5–♭7) to use (in any order or sequence) to suggest the Dorian "color." The rest of the lick completes the Dorian statement as it highlights the 6th degree (F♯).

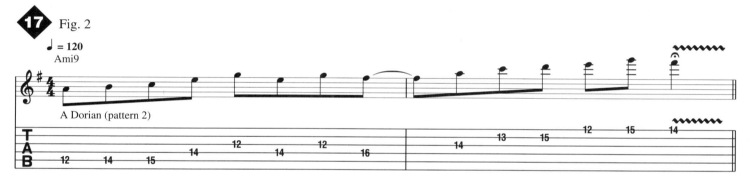

The A Dorian lick in **Fig. 3** superimposes a pair of arpeggios (F♯mi7♭5 and Cma7) to help navigate the sometimes difficult terrain of pattern 1. The method behind this madness is that the F♯mi7♭5 (F♯–A–C–E) is the harmony of the VI chord in A Dorian, and the Cma7 (C–E–G–B) is the ♭III. String them together, and every note in A Dorian is represented.

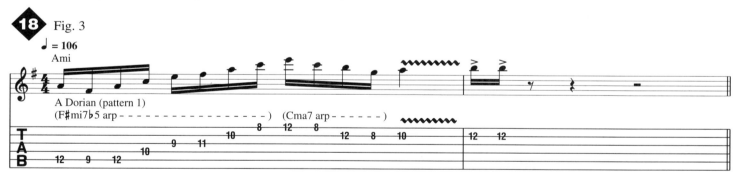

The half-step bends in **Fig. 4** help to bring out the bluesy quality of C Dorian.

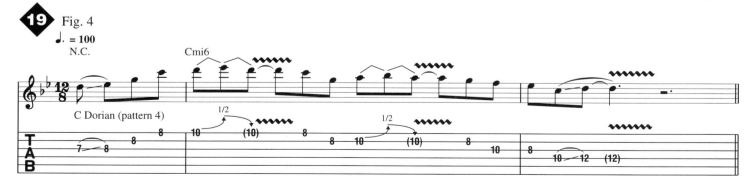

Dorian Applications

The above licks demonstrate that the Dorian mode works well over minor chord types in a solitary situation. But to use it haphazardly over minor chords that are part of a progression can be a dangerous business. Here are some guidelines for determining the application of Dorian in chord progressions.

The II Chord in Major

As discussed in "The Theory of the Modes," each step of the major scale can be represented by a harmonized chord and a mode. This means that for every diatonic chord in a major key, there is a corresponding mode that will provide the "safest" note choices. Therefore, musically speaking, Dorian (second mode) goes hand-in-hand with the II chord in major-key chord progressions (e.g., G Dorian over a Gmi chord in F major; E Dorian over an Emi9 chord in D major, etc.). **Fig. 5** provides a musical example. The key is C major—Cma7 is the I chord, and Dmi7 is the IImi. A simple chord-tone statement provides the melody under the Cma7 chord, while the Dmi7 measure hosts a classic D Dorian phrase. As an experiment, play the melody unaccompanied to see if you can "hear" the chord changes.

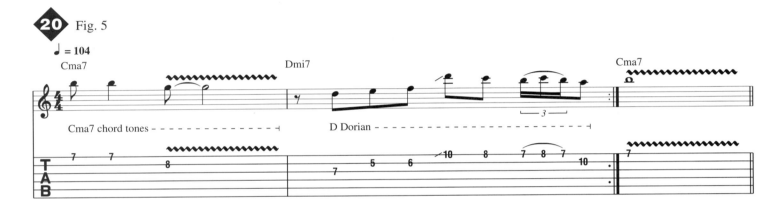

The IV Chord in Minor

Just as there is a designated mode for each chord in a major-key progression, there's a modal choice for each chord in a minor progression. (Refer to "Minor Scale Harmony" in the Aeolian chapter.) In minor key progressions, Dorian belongs to the IVmi chord (e.g., A Dorian over an Ami7 chord in an E minor progression; C Dorian over a Cmi chord in the key of G minor, etc.). **Fig. 6** sheds light on this rule with a typical Imi–IVmi progression in B minor. In the first measure, the B minor pentatonic scale is used to outline the I chord (Bmi), giving way to a strong E Dorian phrase that nails the IV chord (Emi) in the second measure.

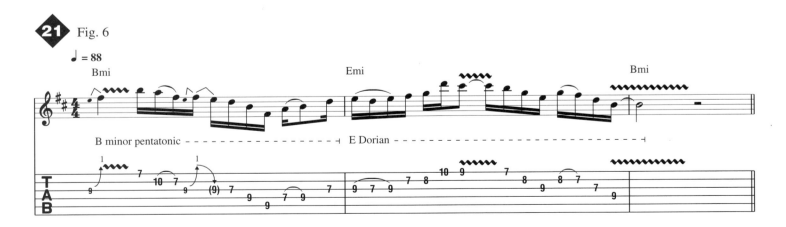

Dorian Progressions

In the "real world" of music, there are many progressions that fall outside the realm of major and minor scale harmony. That is to say, they neither "revolve" around the I chord of a major scale nor the I chord of natural minor. Modal progressions fall into this alternative category of key centers.

In simple terms, a modal progression is a set of related changes that revolve around the I chord of a specific mode. (Refer to "Modes and Modal Progressions" in the "Theory" chapter.) These chords all have to belong to the same mode, and they usually include (in addition to the I) either the II, IV, or VI, or all three. Some of the most common modal progressions are Dorian progressions, and of these, the most common contains only two chords: the Imi and the IV. **Fig. 7** is a classic example of this type of Dorian progression, teamed with the Dorian mode, in the style of one of its greatest benefactors, Carlos Santana.

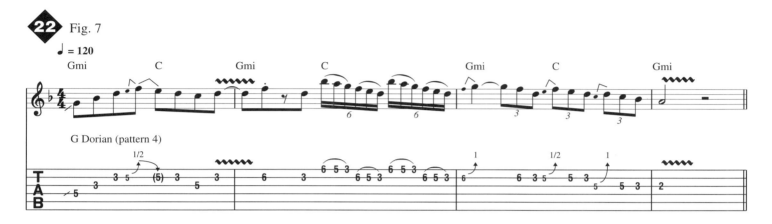

The "key" is G Dorian, and the notes used are clearly derived from the G Dorian mode. This brings to light an important point: When soloing over modal progressions, many players tend to use a "key center" approach—developing melodies from the mode itself as opposed to trying to trying to out-line the chord tones of each change.

Fig. 8 is a jazzy A Dorian progression (Imi–IImi–♭III) featuring another approach to "key center" playing" over a modal progression, this time using the A Dorian mode.

When you develop the ability to recognize modal progressions on the spot, you start to discover "mini modal progressions" lurking within common, run-of-the-mill major progressions. For instance, you're likely to come across the Imi–IVma (Gmi–C) progression in Fig. 7 serving as a II–V move in the key of F major somewhere in your improvisational lifetime. Therefore, you'll know you can dish out your G Dorian licks over both chords. Likewise, the Imi–IImi–♭III (Ami7–Bmi7–Cma7) might eventually pop up in a G major progression serving a IImi–IIImi–IVma function, signaling your chance to simplify the changes by deploying the A Dorian mode over all of the chords.

Odds and Ends

Here's a list of additional tips for creating your own Dorian licks. They're all in A Dorian so you can use them on the Play-Along Progression that follows. When you have them down, transpose them to other keys. Be aware that when applying them, you need to establish the root of Dorian as the pitch axis.

1. Combine Ami7 and Bmi7 arpeggios (together, they account for every note in A Dorian).
2. Combine B minor pentatonic licks with A Dorian.
3. Borrow ideas from the parent scale of G major (harmonized third and/or sixth dyads, open-string licks, etc.).
4. Borrow ideas from the relative minor of the parent scale (E minor).

Play-Along Progression

Use the five patterns of Dorian, located at the top of this chapter, to jam over this A Dorian progression. You can use any of the tips in the "Odds and Ends" section as they are all in A Dorian. Also, try to apply some of the licks in this chapter, changing the rhythms and transposing them where necessary.

Phrygian

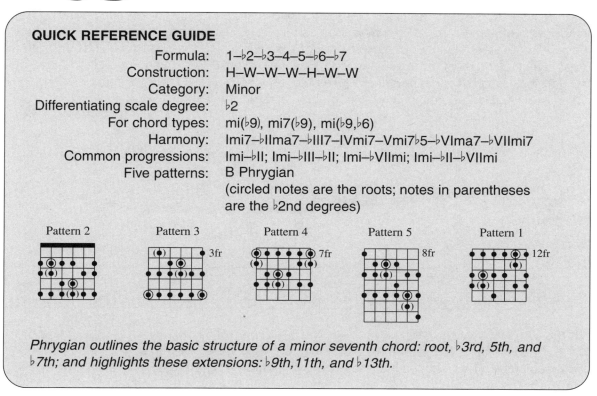

QUICK REFERENCE GUIDE

Formula:	1–♭2–♭3–4–5–♭6–♭7
Construction:	H–W–W–W–H–W–W
Category:	Minor
Differentiating scale degree:	♭2
For chord types:	mi(♭9), mi7(♭9), mi(♭9,♭6)
Harmony:	Imi7–♭IIma7–♭III7–IVmi7–Vmi7♭5–♭VIma7–♭VIImi7
Common progressions:	Imi–♭II; Imi–♭III–♭II; Imi–♭VIImi; Imi–♭II–♭VIImi
Five patterns:	B Phrygian
	(circled notes are the roots; notes in parentheses are the ♭2nd degrees)

Pattern 2 · Pattern 3 (3fr) · Pattern 4 (7fr) · Pattern 5 (8fr) · Pattern 1 (12fr)

Phrygian outlines the basic structure of a minor seventh chord: root, ♭3rd, 5th, and ♭7th; and highlights these extensions: ♭9th, 11th, and ♭13th.

The "Exotic" Minor Mode

Phrygian (1–♭2–♭3–4–5–♭6–♭7), like Dorian, is also categorized as a minor mode because of its ♭3rd degree, but the two modes are miles apart in their overall tonality. The "heavy" ♭6th degree of Phrygian brings it closer in quality to the Aeolian mode, but the startling, "exotic" sound of its ♭2nd degree sets it quite apart from both Dorian and Aeolian. While Phrygian can often be found in the adventurous progressions of jazz/fusion, it also makes its home in the rock world. Featured prominently in the "Middle Eastern" jams of vintage psychedelic bands like Jefferson Airplane and Quicksilver Messenger Service, Phrygian is also a mainstay in the music of mainstream metal bands such as Metallica and Megadeth, and is often the launching point for the riffage of modern metal bands like Korn and the Deftones.

When isolated, Phrygian's tonality is unusual to say the least, but it can be pleasingly melodic when used in its diatonic context—over the IIImi chord in a major progression (**Fig. 1**).

25 Fig. 1

♩ = 96

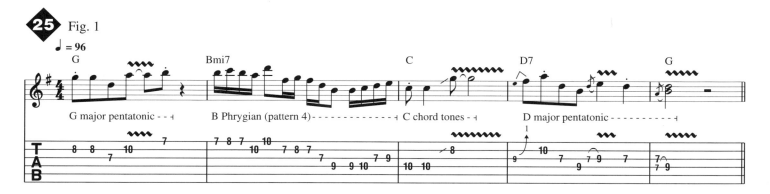

While the melody relies on major pentatonics for the I, IV, and V chords (G, C, and D7), the Phrygian mode is used to outline the basic chord tones of the Bmi7 (B–D–F♯–A) and its diatonic alterations (♭9, ♭13 or ♭6). The result is a "no-surprises" melodic phrase, and although pleasing, the dramatic properties of the mode are suppressed. But when Phrygian is featured in a one-chord vamp, a modal progression, or superimposed over certain chords, its impact is undeniable.

Superimposing Phrygian

Webster's Dictionary definition of *superimpose* is, "to put, stack, or lay on something else." The superimposing of a scale or mode is perhaps best explained as, laying a scale on top of a chord where supposedly it doesn't belong. For example, in Fig. 1 we witnessed that Phrygian "lines up" with the IIImi chord so well that it almost goes by unnoticed. But superimpose Phrygian over a stand-alone major chord, and the result is quite different. For example, the cadenza lick in **Fig. 2** superimposes E Phrygian over an E chord, resulting in a "flamenco" or Spanish flavor.

This next example of superimposing Phrygian (**Fig. 3**) begins with an A natural minor (A Aeolian) sequence which segues into the A Phrygian mode. This represents a mixing, or juggling, of parallel modes (different modes that share the same root), a very useful and highly effective device for soloing over one-chord progressions.

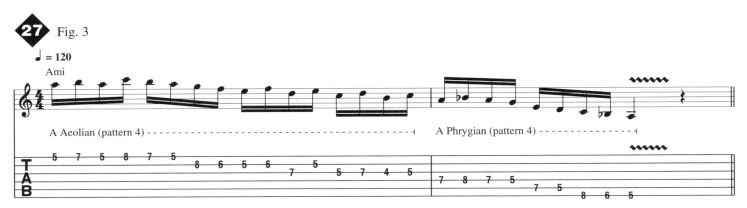

In minor progressions, Phrygian finds its diatonic home on the Vmi chord (refer to "Minor Scale Harmony" in the Aeolian chapter), but it can also be very useful when superimposed over the V7 chord in a major progression. The II–V–I, C major progression in **Fig. 4** offers an example of this process.

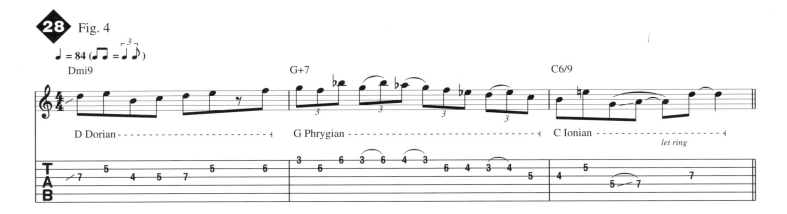

D Dorian on the IImi chord (Dmi9) and C Ionian on the I (C6/9) supply the consonant note choices for those melodic statements. On the V chord (G+7) however, dissonance or tension is added with the application of the G Phrygian mode, highlighting both the ♭9 and ♯9 (A♭ and B♭), and the ♭13 (E♭)—or ♭6—of the chord.

Be aware that when used this way, the Phrygian mode does not supply the 3rd of the V chord, but when followed up with a strong resolving phrase on the I chord, it can function very well as an altered scale.

Phrygian Progressions and Riffs

In the genres of fusion and heavy metal, the harmonized chords from the Phrygian mode are often used as a backdrop to support adventurous soloing explorations. In heavy metal, these progressions generally employ power chords and tend to be riff-oriented, whereas fusion takes advantage of the richer quality of seventh and extended chords. The progression in **Fig. 5** uses chords harmonized from the A Phrygian mode: Imi (Ami7), ♭II (B♭ma9), and ♭VIImi (Gmi13). All the extensions are diatonic to the mode, making the progression ripe for an A Phrygian blow-fest.

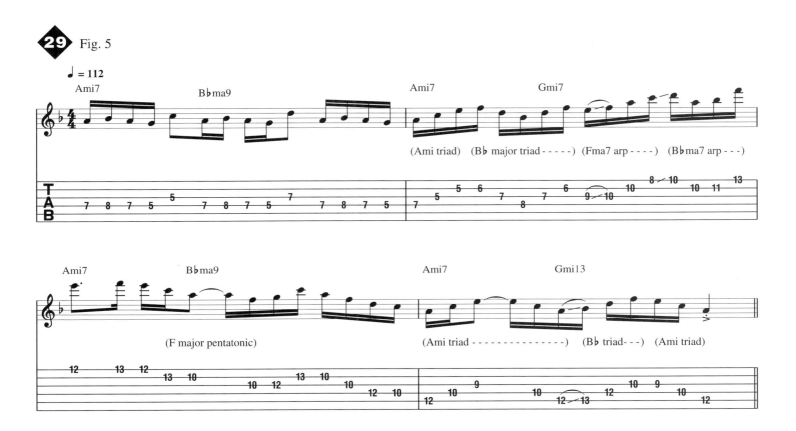

All of the note choices in Fig. 5 are derived from the A Phrygian mode. Measure 1 features a rhythmic displacement of a melodic motif. The second measure exploits the triads and arpeggios based off of the root (Ami triad), ♭2nd (B♭ triad and B♭ma7 arpeggio), and ♭6th (Fma7 arpeggio) degrees of the mode. In measure 3, the major pentatonic form of A Phrygian's parent scale (F major) provides a nice break in the action, and measure 4 slips back-and-forth between the Imi (Ami) and ♭II (B♭) triads.

Fig. 6 represents a heavy-metal version of an A Phrygian progression. Riff-oriented and of a sinister quality, it employs the harmonized power chords of the root, ♭2nd, 5th, ♭6th, and ♭7th degrees of the scale: A5, B♭5, E(♭5), F5, and G5.

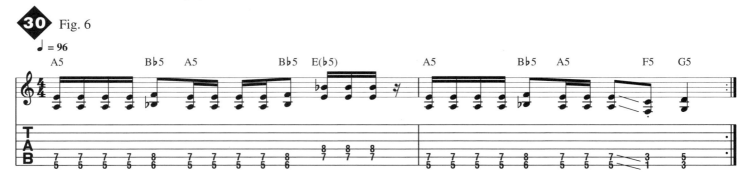

Fig. 7 is a modern-metal riff derived from E Phrygian. Ardent and foreboding, it displays the extremely heavy prospects of the Phrygian mode.

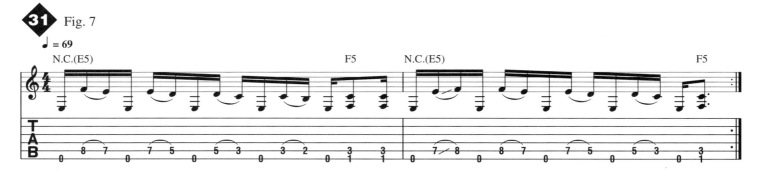

Odds and Ends

Here's a list of additional tips for creating your own Phrygian licks. They're all in B Phrygian so you can use them on the Play-Along Progression that follows. When you have them down, transpose them to other keys. Be aware that when applying them, you need to establish the root of Phrygian as the pitch axis.

1. Play parallel minor pentatonic licks and add the ♭2 and ♭6 (i.e., B minor pentatonic, adding C and G notes).
2. Play the Vmi7♭5 arpeggio (F♯mi7♭5) and resolve to the root of Phrygian.
3. Borrow ideas from the parent scale (G major).
4. Borrow ideas from the relative minor of the parent scale (E minor).

Play-Along Progression

Use the five patterns of Phrygian, located at the top of this chapter, to jam over this B Phrygian progression. You can use any of the tips in the "Odds and Ends" section as they are all in B Phrygian. Also, try to apply some of the licks in this chapter, changing the rhythms and transposing them where necessary.

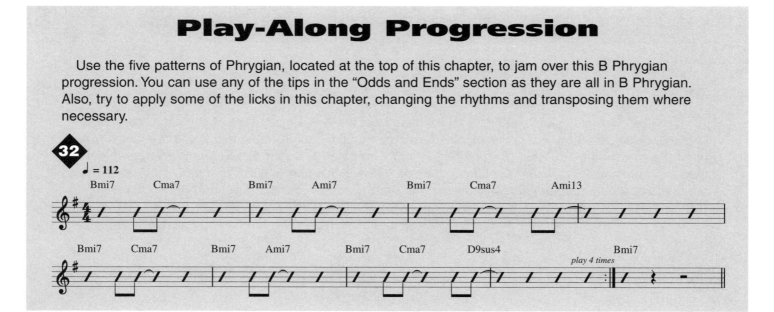

Lydian

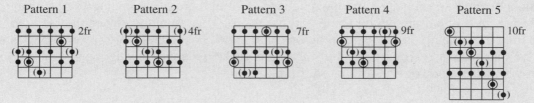
The "Dreamy" Major Mode

Of all the modes, Lydian (1–2–3–#4–5–6–7) is the closest in structure to that of the major scale, or Ionian mode. Both modes contain the same major pentatonic framework (1–2–3–5–6) and share a major 7th—or leading tone—scale degree. The only thing that sets Lydian apart from Ionian is its raised, or sharped, 4th degree, but this one difference is significant. The #4 creates a series of three whole steps from the root which in turn establishes a sense of mystery.

Whereas Ionian is consonant and familiar, Lydian has a "dreamy" and anticipatory nature. Indeed, sometimes it's difficult to establish the tonal center when Lydian is employed—almost like there are two tonic notes simultaneously in play. Often used as the musical backdrop for the wide-eyed wonder of childhood in movies, Lydian is also a favorite choice among singer/songwriters like Fleetwood Mac's Stevie Nicks ("Dreams," "Sara") and Joni Mitchell, who use it to paint atmospheric settings for their lyrics. And in the hands of master guitarists like Joe Satriani and Steve Vai, the Lydian mode can bring tears to a listener's eyes.

Lydian Applications

Lydian is the fourth mode of the major scale, making it the natural choice for the IV chord in a major progression. When applied over the IV chord, its effect can be subtle, but if the #4 of the mode is featured prominently, it adds a #11 quality to the chord. To some players, this extension is a little too unsettling or active, so they avoid it. But others enjoy its "emotion evoking" capabilities and use it often. The I–IV, A major progression in **Fig. 1** puts D Lydian in its diatonic setting over the IV chord (Dsus2), but the strategically placed #4 (G#) brings out a #11 quality in the chord even though that extension is not present. Notice the yearning, somewhat heartbreaking mood the line instills.

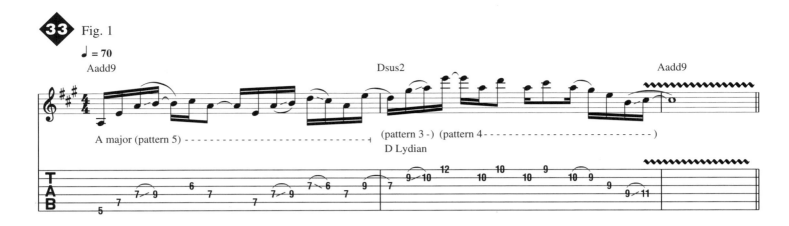

33 Fig. 1

In minor progressions, the Lydian mode finds its diatonic home on the often encountered ♭VI chord. (Refer to "Minor Scale Harmony" in the Aeolian chapter.) Many players find the mode easier to apply in these "minor" surroundings. Perhaps because in major progressions the ♯4 of Lydian (played over the IV chord) is enharmonic (the same note) to the 7th degree of the key center—a notoriously difficult note to use in soloing. But in minor progressions, the ♯4 of Lydian (over the ♭VI chord) is enharmonic to the much used 2nd degree of the key center, making it sound a little more "familiar" to the ear. **Fig. 2** offers an example over an F♯ minor rock progression.

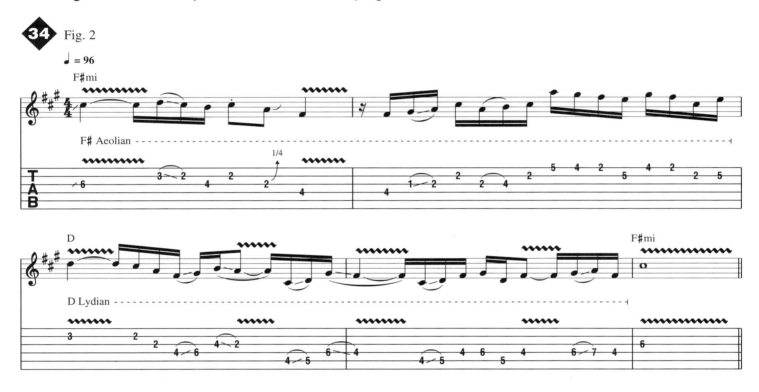

34 Fig. 2

The lines over the Imi chord (F♯mi) are constructed from the F♯ natural minor scale (F♯ Aeolian), and D Lydian is applied over the ♭VI (D). Notice that the G♯ (2nd degree of the key center) is featured prominently in the second measure of the Imi chord. This "familiarizes" the listener to the note, resulting in a less startling effect when it functions as the ♯4 of D Lydian in the following measures.

The Lydian mode really sparkles when it has a chance to "breathe." It's for this reason many players use the harmonized chords from Lydian to write progressions expressly made for the exploitation of the mode itself. (Refer to "Modes and Modal Progressions" in the "Theory" chapter.) **Fig. 3** places the I (A), II7 (B7), and IIImi (C♯mi) chords of A Lydian over an A bass-note pedal, inviting every note from the mode to be used at will. The important chord here is the recurring II chord (B7) as it contains the ♯4 (D♯) of A Lydian. You'll find progressions like this in the instrumental guitar-rock style of players such as Joe Satriani and Steve Vai.

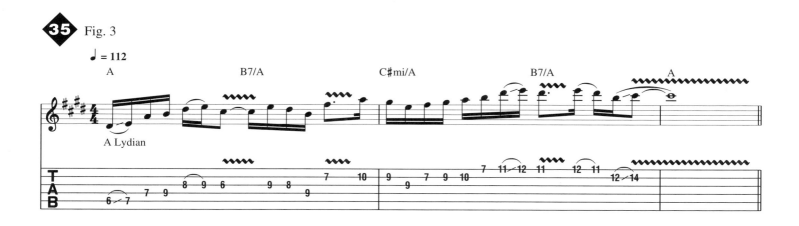

35 Fig. 3

Some players are so attuned to the Lydian mode they use it as an alternative to Ionian. The progression in **Fig. 4** is a common I–IV in C major. The diatonic source for melodies is C Ionian on the I chord (Cma7) and F Lydian on the IV (Fma7), but here Lydian is used out of context—or superimposed—over the I chord. Interestingly, this tends to place more emphasis on the "diatonic" F Lydian lines.

36 Fig. 4

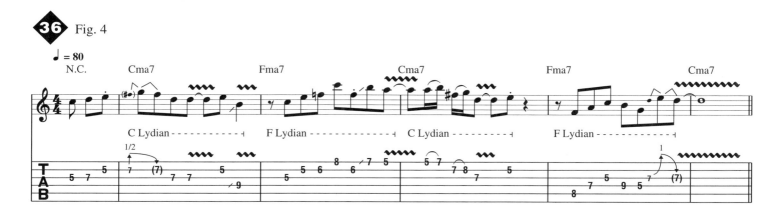

To the unaccustomed ear, lines like this are too "outside" the key center. Like fine wine, one needs to develop an acquired taste for some applications of the Lydian mode.

Borrowing From the Parent Scale

Relating a mode to its parent scale and "borrowing" fingering patterns, licks, arpeggios, and even chords from that scale, is common practice among experienced modal players. Since the Lydian mode is so similar in construction and application to the major scale (Ionian), it often receives the "parent scale" treatment. For instance, when playing D Lydian, some guitarists use licks they have developed from the three-notes-per-string pattern 5 of the A major scale (parent scale of D Lydian). The "starting" and "ending" notes of their phrases sometimes need slight adjustment, but the process puts their fingers in familiar territory on the fretboard.

The following three examples are "parent scale concepts." They're all in D Lydian, to get you primed for the Lydian play-along progression on the CD.

The D Lydian lick in **Fig. 5** scatters the notes of an Ama7 arpeggio—the tonic chord of the parent scale of A major—around a pair of F# "target" notes. Though not part of an Ama7 arpeggio, F# is the 3rd of the Dma7 chord and helps to keep the melodic focus on the chord.

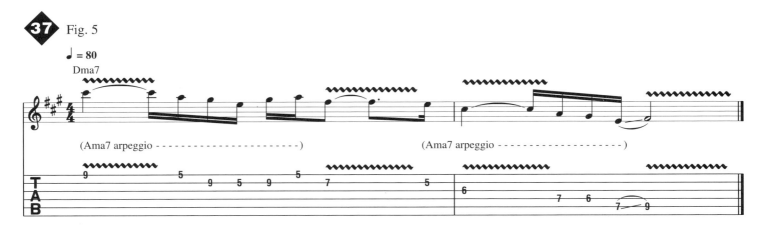

Fig. 5

The **Fig. 6** D Lydian/parent scale example draws on the concept of playing minor pentatonics off the 3rd degree of the major scale (see "Odds and Ends" in the Ionian chapter). Again, in this situation A major is the parent scale, and C# is the 3rd degree of A major. Comfortably snuggled in the lick-laden C# minor pentatonic scale, this example is representative of the pentatonic double-stop stylings of Jimi Hendrix. Using the minor pentatonic scale pattern in this way (1/2 step below the root of a major chord) affords some "automatic" moves that outline five choice Lydian notes (2–3–#4–6–7), while omitting only the root and 5th.

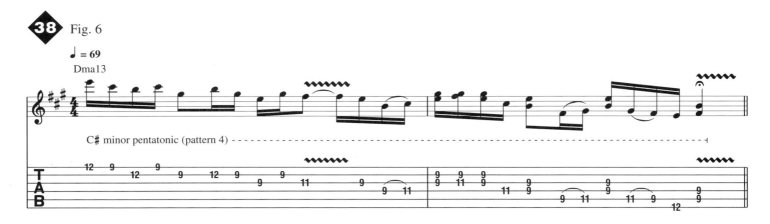

Fig. 6

Fig. 7 is a fusion-style D Lydian lick that superimposes the I (A), IV (D), and V (E) major triads from the parent scale of A major. Played over a basic D chord, the A triad reflects a Dma9 quality, the D nails the chord tones, while the E drives home the D Lydian tonality as it contains the colorful 2nd, #4th, and 6th degrees of the mode.

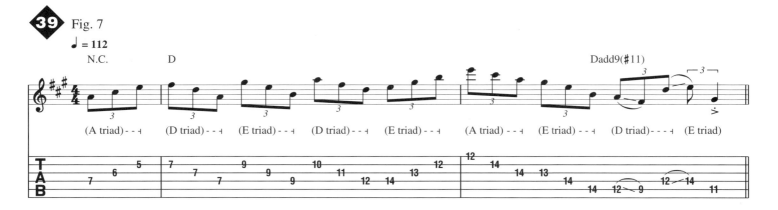

Fig. 7

Odds and Ends

Here's a list of additional tips for creating your own Lydian licks. They're all in D Lydian so you can use them on the Play-Along Progression that follows. When you have them down, transpose them to other keys. Be aware that when applying them, you need to establish the root of Lydian as the pitch axis.

1. Add a G# (#4) to a Dma7 arpeggio.
2. Play D major pentatonics and add a G# (#4).
3. Move around the neck using patterns of A major (the parent scale).
4. Move around the neck using patterns of F# minor (relative minor of parent scale).
5. Play B Dorian Licks (second mode of parent scale) and accentuate the 6th degree (G#, which is the #4 of D Lydian).
6. Combine F#mi7 and G#mi7♭5 arpeggios. (VI and VII chords of parent scale, they highlight the 3rd and #4th degrees of Lydian.)

Play-Along Progression

Use the five patterns of Lydian, located at the top of this chapter, to jam over this D Lydian progression. You can use any of the tips in the "Odds and Ends" section as they are all in D Lydian. Also, try to apply some of the licks in this chapter, changing the rhythms and transposing them where necessary.

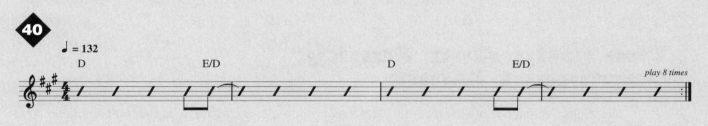

Mixolydian

The "Hip And Funky" Dominant Mode

Mixolydian, the fifth mode, is placed in the major mode category simply because of its major 3rd degree. But unlike its sister modes—Ionian and Lydian—Mixolydian contains a ♭7th degree (1–2–3–4–5–6–♭7), setting it apart and placing it in a category all by itself. Referred to by many as the "dominant mode," Mixolydian aligns perfectly with dominant seventh chords: The root, 3rd, 5th, and ♭7th scale degrees of the mode outline the basic chord structure, while the remaining notes nail the routinely applied extensions of the 9th (2nd), 13th (6th), and 11th (4th). (The latter usually serves a dom7sus4 function.)

The "sound" of Mixolydian is in the music all around us. The abundance of dominant seventh chords used in the progressions of blues, funk, jazz, country, and rock, make Mixolydian a popular choice among soloists in those styles. The mode is also used heavily by songwriters wishing for a "hipper" or "funkier" alternative to the "prettier" Ionian mode. And many a classic riff is Mixolydian by nature—Roy Orbison's "Oh, Pretty Woman," the Beatles' "I Feel Fine" and "Birthday," Jimi Hendrix's "Third Stone from the Sun," and Miles Davis's "All Blues," to name only a few.

Mixolydian Licks

Like all the modes (except Locrian), if you chip away at Mixolydian you'll find a familiar underlying pentatonic framework. Removal of the ♭7th and the 4th degrees of Mixolydian leaves the major pentatonic scale (1–2–3–5–6). Many players use this process to establish a common-ground area on the neck where the two scales can "intermingle." **Fig. 1** offers an example of this pentatonic-meets-Mixolydian approach in the fail-safe, C major pentatonic pattern in 5th position (relative A minor pentatonic). Most of the lick consists of commonplace C major pentatonic moves, but the occasional B♭ and F notes add the Mixolydian spice.

Fig. 1

♩ = 126

C7

C major pentatonic/ Mixolydian (pattern 3)

Many guitarists struggle for a long time trying to get Mixolydian to "sound right" to their ears. Often the problem lies in the way they are phrasing their notes—either melodically, rhythmically, or both. The C Mixolydian lick in **Fig. 2** is one example of balancing rhythmic and melodic phrasing. The simple descending melody in the first measure is set against the super-funk syncopation of sixteenth-note rhythms. In the second measure, the rhythms relax and give way to the melody which is considerably more involved than it was in the first bar.

Fig. 2

♩ = 92

C9

C Mixolydian (pattern 4)

Fig. 3 represents another approach to phrasing. Rhythmic variation takes a back seat while speed and flash take over to drive this E Mixolydian sequence. Too fast for the listener to cue into each and every pitch, the line depends on note targeting for melodic interest. The lick starts on the ♭7th—the magical note of Mixolydian—and ends on the root, but that's not all there is by a long shot. Attention has been given to the first note in each grouping to make sure they add up to a melodic, E Mixolydian statement. In order, they are D–G♯–A–D–E–A–B–E. Rearrange them, and you'll get the notes of an E7 chord (E–G♯–B–D)—the I chord in E Mixolydian—plus a few left-over A notes. But the A notes are hardly throwaways—they represent the suspended-fourth sound—an important ingredient of Mixolydian.

Fig. 3

♩ = 144

E

E Mixolydian (pattern 2)

In the II–V–I progressions of improvisational jazz, the V chord is usually treated with some form of alteration (see "Phrygian" chapter, Fig. 4). But when an "inside" melodic statement is called for, Mixolydian reigns supreme as the diatonic choice in major keys. **Fig. 4** gives an example of Mixolydian and two other modes in play over a II–V–I in B♭ major. On the IImi chord (Cmi7), the C Dorian mode is dispatched, which leads to a smooth transition into F Mixolydian on the V chord (F7). Notice how the first part of this phrase outlines an F7 arpeggio (I chord in F Mixolydian). This segues to a simple run up the first five notes of F Mixolydian, and the melody ends on a B♭ma7 arpeggio (I chord in B♭ Ionian). All of the notes in this three-measure example belong to the key of B-flat major, but the way they are phrased leaves no doubt that modes are in play.

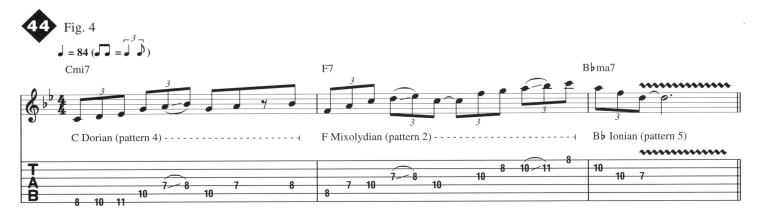

Fig. 4

Fig. 5 is a V–I, C major progression in a samba vein. The double stops—or dyads—are thirds harmonized from the G Mixolydian mode, with a final resolution to the root and 3rd of a C chord. These types of lines can be easy to apply if you know your diatonic thirds in major keys—just borrow from the parent scale of the mode your are in. In this example, you can think of thirds in the key of C major, as it's the parent scale of G Mixolydian. Be aware that when you are borrowing from the parent scale, your "home base"—or tonic resting point—shifts. For instance, in this example, the first two dyads are "home-base" positions for a G major chord, while the last two fit a C chord.

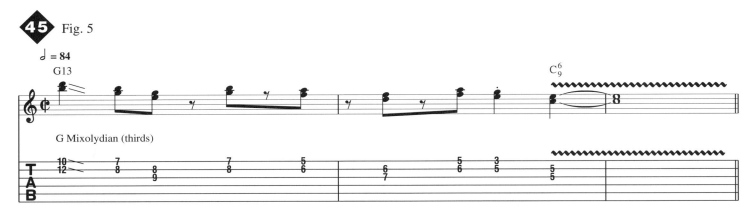

Fig. 5

Fig. 6 harmonizes G Mixolydian again, but this time in sixth intervals. It's a country style, hybrid-picking (pick-and-fingers) lick, featuring an array of hammer-ons from the open G and D strings. Each hammered-on note is the bottom of a sixth-interval couplet. Again, it's often easier to create lines like these by borrowing from the parent scale.

Fig. 6

Mixolydian and the Blues

The wealth of dominant seventh chords found in blues music offers many enticing opportunities for Mixolydian-lovers. Consequently, many blues guitarists draw from the mode extensively, but not in the conventional manner. In blues, the Mixolydian mode is usually heard in conjunction with that style's intrinsic scale—the blues scale (1–♭3–4–♭5–5–♭7). What many guitarists do is "graft" the two scales into one, creating what is referred to as a "hybrid scale."

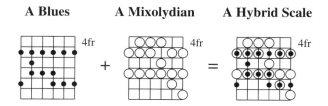

The diagram illustrates what happens when you "plop" the A blues scale on top of A Mixolydian (the dots represent the blues-scale notes, the circles make up the Mixolydian mode). The fret areas that share a dot *and* a circle represent the common tones of the two scales—the root, 4th, 5th, and ♭7th—a rather ambiguous set of notes that could imply either a dominant seventh or a minor seventh chord. The five notes that surround this basic framework are the ones that truly dictate the tonality at any given time. Mixolydian supplies the 2nd, 3rd, and 6th, while the blues scale supplies the ♭3rd and ♭5th—the "blue" notes. The end result is a nearly-chromatic, nine-note scale (1–2–♭3–3–4–♭5–5–6–♭7) known as the "Mixolydian/blues hybrid scale," pictured here in patterns 4 and 2.

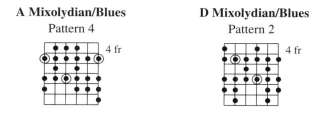

Don't spend a lot of practice time running up and down these patterns, as this is not the way the Mixolydian/blues hybrid scale is generally used. The object is to see and feel it as two overlapping patterns, and to juggle phrases from each, thus molding them into one, push-and-pull, hybrid sound. **Fig. 7** features an array of Mixolydian/blues hybrid moves carved from patterns 4 and 2, over a condensed I–IV–V dominant blues progression. (NOTE: In this example, the Mixolydian/blues hybrid scale is transposed and used over each change, mainly for demonstration purposes. Until you get a handle on it, practice using it only over the I chord in dominant blues progressions.)

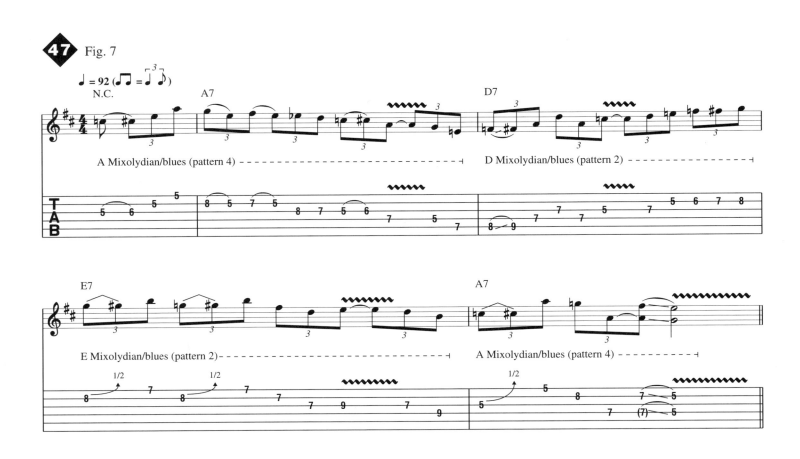

47 Fig. 7

Fig. 8 is a jazz-blues example of the B♭ Mixolydian/blues hybrid scale in action. When constructing your own hybrid scale licks in a traditional jazz style, remember to use slides in place of bends.

48 Fig. 8

The blues-rock example in **Fig. 9** illustrates the perfect pairing of the E Mixolydian/blues hybrid scale with the "mother of all blues-rock chords," E7♯9. The major and minor 3rds of the scale align with the 3rd and the ♯9 of the chord, while the ♭5 tempers the lick with just the right amount of "meanness."

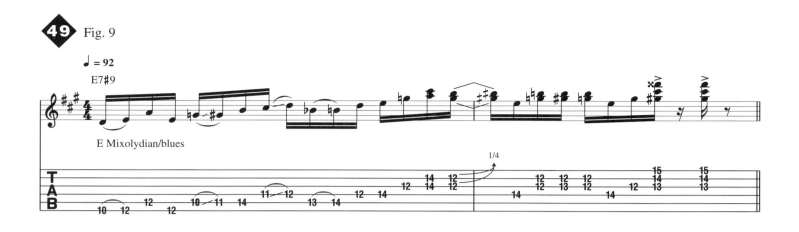

Odds and Ends

Here's a list of additional tips for creating your own Mixolydian licks. They're all in C Mixolydian so you can use them on the Play-Along Progression that follows. When you have them down, transpose them to other keys. Be aware that when applying them, you need to establish the root of Mixolydian as the pitch axis.

1. Use your C Dorian licks but replace the minor 3rds (E♭) with major 3rds (E).
2. Add an F, D, or A note to a C7 arpeggio for the following results: C7add4–C9–C13.
3. Use chromatic passing tones (ascending and descending) to bridge all of the whole steps (C–C♯–D; D–D♯–E; G–G♭–F; B♭–B–C; etc.).
4. Play an Emi7♭5 arpeggio (VII chord of parent scale) and resolve to C. Experiment using other arpeggios from the parent scale (B♭ma7, Fma7, Dmi7, etc.).
5. Play C, B♭, and F triads (V, IV, and I triads from parent scale).
6. Play C Mixolydian over a one-measure II–V change in F major.

Play-Along Progression

Use the five patterns of Mixolydian, located at the top of this chapter, to jam over this C Mixolydian progression. You can use any of the tips in the "Odds and Ends" section as they are all in C Mixolydian. Also, try to apply some of the licks in this chapter, changing the rhythms and transposing them where necessary.

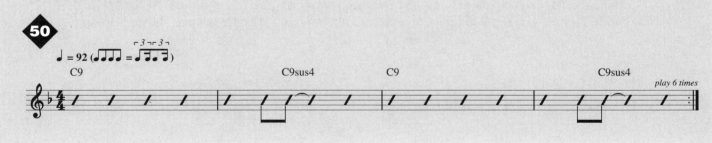

Aeolian

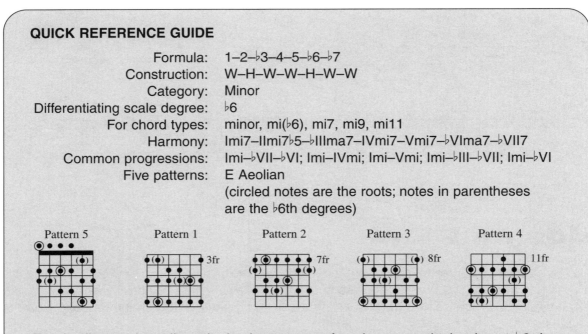

QUICK REFERENCE GUIDE

Formula:	1–2–♭3–4–5–♭6–♭7
Construction:	W–H–W–W–H–W–W
Category:	Minor
Differentiating scale degree:	♭6
For chord types:	minor, mi(♭6), mi7, mi9, mi11
Harmony:	Imi7–IImi7♭5–♭IIIma7–IVmi7–Vmi7–♭VIma7–♭VII7
Common progressions:	Imi–♭VII–♭VI; Imi–IVmi; Imi–Vmi; Imi–♭III–♭VII; Imi–♭VI
Five patterns:	E Aeolian
	(circled notes are the roots; notes in parentheses are the ♭6th degrees)

Pattern 5   Pattern 1   Pattern 2   Pattern 3   Pattern 4

The Aeolian mode outlines the basic structure of a minor seventh chord: root, ♭3rd, 5th, and ♭7th; and these extensions: 9th, 11th, and ♭13th.

The "Romantic" Minor Mode

Aeolian, often called the "romantic" minor mode (the first twelve notes of the theme from the film "The Godfather" speak volumes), is simply the modal name for the natural minor scale (1–2–♭3–4–5–♭6–♭7). While relegated as the sixth mode of the major scale, it is the "king daddy" of the minor mode category (Aeolian, Dorian, Phrygian, and Locrian), and of all other minor scales (including melodic minor and harmonic minor—see "Other Modes" chapter). Since it is one-and-the-same with the natural minor scale, Aeolian also serves as the basis of minor scale harmony. So before we get into licks and applications, let's have a look at harmonizing the Aeolian mode.

Minor Scale Harmony

Just as it did with the major scale, harmonizing every degree of the natural minor scale, or Aeolian mode, results in a predictable series of triad and seventh chord qualities, shown here in E minor:

In fact, these are the same chord qualities found in the major scale, but starting from a different point. While the same can be said for all the harmonized modes—Dorian, Phrygian, etc.—the Aeolian mode's popularity and its status as "the natural minor scale" make it a particularly important frame of reference. Just as you did with the major scale, you should commit this chord order to memory so you will be able to discern minor key progressions.

Also, try to memorize the corresponding mode for each chord in the harmonized scale.

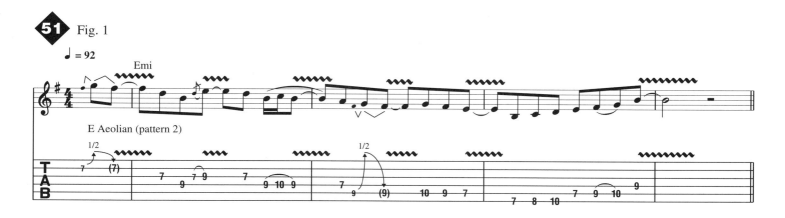

Aeolian Licks and Applications

The Aeolian tonality can be considered as being between Dorian and Phrygian—sharing the soft and melodic 9th (2nd) of the former, and the heavy ♭6th of the latter. Therefore, to analyze a melody as being Aeolian means that it has a minor 3rd of course, but most importantly the combination of the ♭6th and 9th (2nd). The simple E Aeolian melody in **Fig. 1** showcases these three notes in a bluesy example that discloses the haunting aspects of the mode. The half-step bends heighten the crying quality produced by the pairing of the 2nd with the ♭3rd (F♯ and G), while the frequent ♭6ths (C) add an atmosphere of suspense.

51 Fig. 1

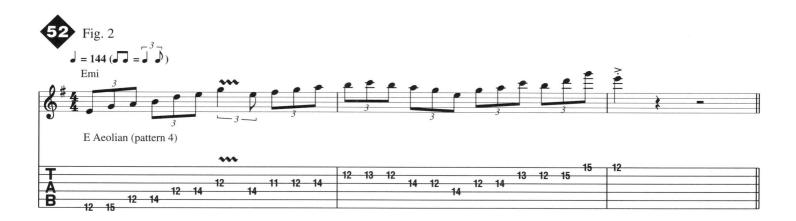

The blues-rock example in **Fig. 2** is basically a sequenced run up the E minor pentatonic scale (E–G–A–B–D), the basic framework of the E Aeolian mode. The brief inclusions of the "missing" scale degrees—♭6th (C) and 2nd (F♯)—give the lick its Aeolian flavor.

52 Fig. 2

Fig. 3 is a jazzy approach to C Aeolian over a Imi–Vmi vamp. Notice the liberal use of half-step slides from the ♭6th (A♭) and to the ♭3rd (E♭).

The melancholy **Fig. 4** strings together the ♭6th (Fma7) and ♭3rd (Cma7) arpeggios of A Aeolian. The Fma7 draws out the "gloomy" ♭6th degree of the mode while the Cma7 suggests an Ami(add9) quality, which softens the mood.

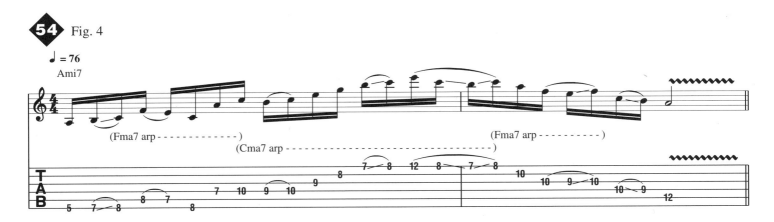

In styles such as fusion and progressive rock, it's not unusual to find guitarists juggling Aeolian, Dorian, and even Phrygian melodies back and forth over an extended Imi chord vamp. **Fig. 5** tosses around ideas from all three of these modes in a two-bar example over an Ami chord.

Using Aeolian in Key Center Playing

There are many approaches to soloing over minor key (Aeolian) progressions. Some guitarists rely exclusively on minor pentatonic scales while others craft melodies using the complete Aeolian mode. There are players who like to arpeggiate the chord tones of changes while others enjoy "filling in the holes" those arpeggios leave behind, by "plugging in" the diatonic mode over each chord. It depends on the style of music, but generally speaking, a mixture of all four of these techniques usually provides the most interesting and melodic results. Let's have a look at some hands-on examples over a few minor progressions.

Fig. 6 is a four-measure progression in the key of D minor: Imi–♭VI–♭VII–Imi. The D Aeolian mode could work over the entire progression, but instead the melody holds back in the first two bars, staying within D minor pentatonic. This anticipates the arrival of the ♭VI and ♭VII chords in measure 3 where the D Aeolian scale is dispatched in a short melodic statement that highlights the chord changes. This "holding-back-on-the-I-chord-approach" can be very effective in adding impact to the arrival of new chord changes.

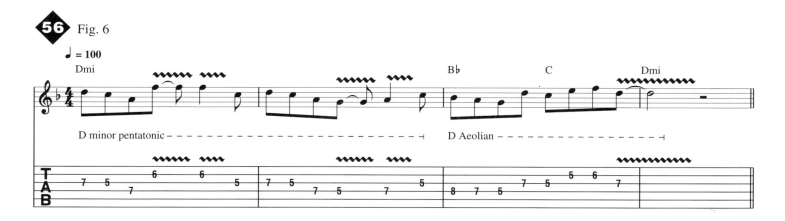

Fig. 7 is basically the same progression as Fig. 6 except it is longer, allowing more time for melodies to be developed over the changes. This being the case, the chord/scale approach is used, exploiting the entire diatonic mode of each chord—Aeolian on the Imi, Lydian on the ♭VI, and Mixolydian on the ♭VII chord. Each two-bar section is a melodic statement in its own right, but there is a definite sense of unity as all the modes are derived from the parent mode, D Aeolian.

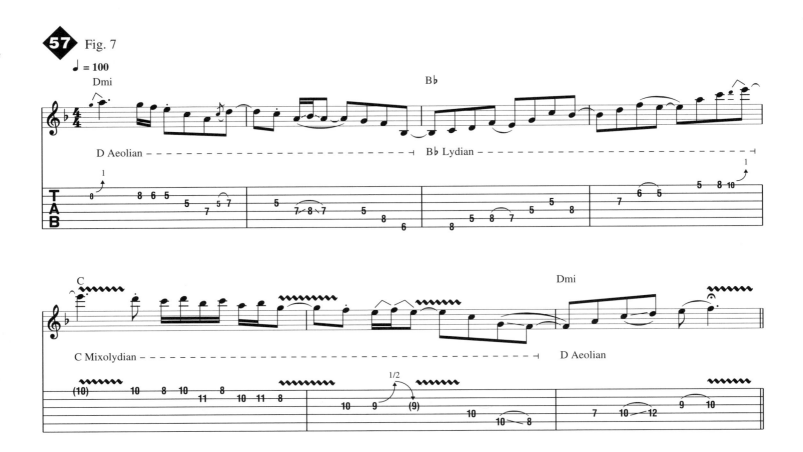

57 Fig. 7

♩ = 100

Fig. 8 is a II–V–I–IV progression in C minor, featuring a mixture of arpeggios and modal playing. All chords are diatonic to C Aeolian except for the V chord, which is dominant instead of minor seventh in quality. However, its ♯5th and ♯9th alterations are diatonic to the key.

The example begins with a Dmi7♭5 arpeggio in the II chord measure, which segues to G Phrygian for the V chord (G+7♯9) change. The mode serves its purpose well as it outlines the ♯9, ♭9, root, ♭7, and ♯5 of the chord, proving itself a useful alternative to the altered scale (refer to the "Other Modes" chapter). C Aeolian note choices color the Imi chord in measure 3, and the example closes with a strong F Dorian statement over the IVmi chord. Again, all the modes chosen for this example belong to the "parent" mode of the progression (in this case, C Aeolian), resulting in a strong sense of continuity.

58 Fig. 8

♩ = 120

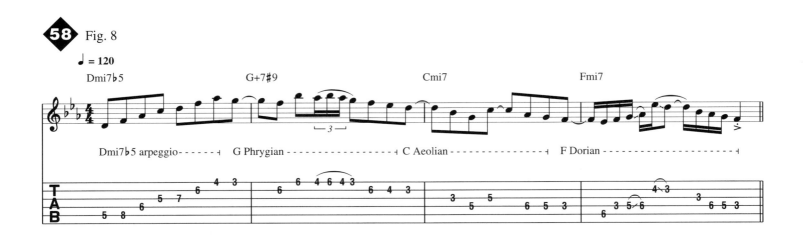

Odds and Ends

Here's a list of additional tips for creating your own Aeolian licks. They're all in E Aeolian so you can use them with the Play-Along Progression that follows. When you have them down, transpose them to other keys. Be aware that when applying them, you need to establish the root of Aeolian as the pitch axis.

1. Play diatonic third and sixth dyads harmonized from G major (parent key).
2. Mix E minor, A minor, and B minor pentatonic scales. Combined, they represent every note of E Aeolian.
3. Mix E, A, and B minor triads (I–IV–V). Combined, they represent every note of E Aeolian.
4. Play a D7 or F♯mi7♭5 arpeggio and resolve to an E minor pentatonic lick.

Play-Along Progression

Use the five patterns of Aeolian, located at the top of this chapter, to jam over this E Aeolian progression. You can use any of the tips in the "Odds and Ends" section as they are all in E Aeolian. Also, try to apply some of the licks in this chapter, changing the rhythms and transposing them where necessary.

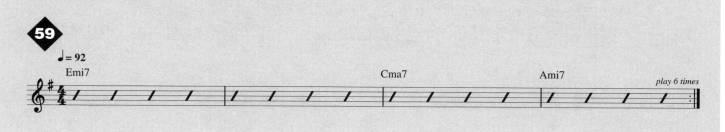

Locrian

The "Eccentric" Diminished Mode

Of all the minor modes of the major scale, Locrian (seventh mode) is the oddball of the bunch. Although its 1–♭2–♭3–4–♭5–♭6–♭7 formula is similar to that of Phrygian (1–♭2–♭3–4–5–♭6–♭7), the ♭5th degree of Locrian pushes the mode "over the top" of the consonant ladder into the further reaches of dissonance. Often called the "diminished" mode (due to its I chord triad harmony: root–♭3–♭5), it's usually associated with mi7♭5 chords. Rarely encountered in major progressions of any music style, mi7♭5 chords usually function as the II chord in the minor keys of jazz and jazz/fusion. Consequently, the Locrian mode is a popular improvisational tool in those idioms. This isn't to say that Locrian doesn't dwell in other music styles. Many heavy-metal guitarists are acutely aware of the sinister properties lurking within the Locrian mode, and progressive-blues guitarists have been known to use it in substitution situations. In the proper context, the Locrian mode can prove to be a valuable ally.

Locrian Applications

Locrian and the mi7♭5 chord form a dream-team combination when placed in the II chord slot of minor progressions in jazz. The mode outlines the chord's basic structure (root–♭3–♭5–♭7) plus adds its diatonic alterations—the ♭9th, and ♯5. The leftover degree (the 4th, or 11th) matches up with the root of the V chord, which almost always follows the IImi7♭5.

Fig. 1 represents an intrinsic fixture in jazz—the minor II–V–I progression. Over the II chord (Bmi7♭5), the B Locrian line rises to the ♭9 (C) then falls to resolve to the root of the V chord (E7♭9). Here the E Phrygian mode is dispatched in a similarly contoured line that also peaks out at the ♭9 (F) of the chord then descends to resolve on the 9th (B) of the I chord (Ami9). Notice how pattern 4 of B Locrian flows into pattern 2 of E Phrygian. The fingering for each is the same because the modes are related—both belonging to the parent mode of A Aeolian.

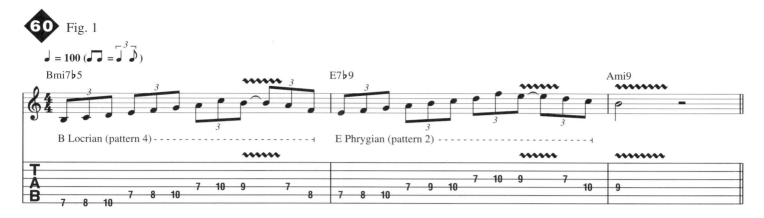

Fig. 1

In the unconventional improvisational world of jazz/fusion, it's not uncommon to encounter a mi7♭5 chord in a static situation (lasting two or more bars, functioning as a "temporary I chord"), as in **Fig. 2**. Even though the Bmi7♭5 is not functioning as a II chord, the B Locrian mode still rises to the occasion. Notice how the hammer/pull moves enhance the "bluesy" quality produced by the pairing of the 4th and ♭5th degrees (E and F).

Fig. 2

In the major-key progressions of pop music, the VII° chord is rarely used. When that harmony is required, a first-inversion V chord is usually substituted in its place. For example: in the key of C major, a G/B chord substitutes for the B° or Bmi7♭5 chord. If you think of the B note as being the root, the chord can be considered a Bmi♯5—a diatonic alteration of the VII chord—making it a candidate for the B Locrian mode. Placed in such a context, the Locrian mode can be extremely melodic. **Fig. 3** offers an example of B Locrian over the first-inversion V chord in a typical C major pop progression.

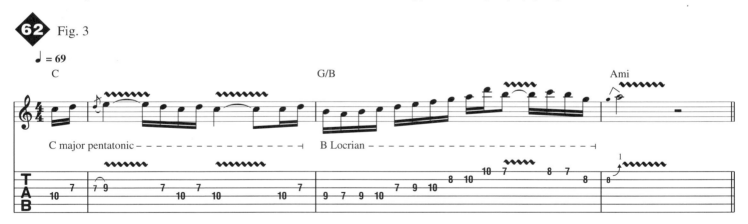

Fig. 3

Because of the super-alteration properties found within the structure of the mode (♭9, ♯9, ♭5, ♯5), many players like to superimpose Locrian over functioning V chords. **Fig. 4** isolates the turnaround bars of a G minor blues progression. In the Imi–IVmi measure (Gmi7–Cmi7), a G minor pentatonic (add9) lick establishes the bluesy mood, then the D Locrian mode takes over on the V chord (D7♯9), hitting every possible alteration. This lick takes full advantage of the blues-scale framework (sans 5th) that lies within the Locrian mode.

63 Fig. 4

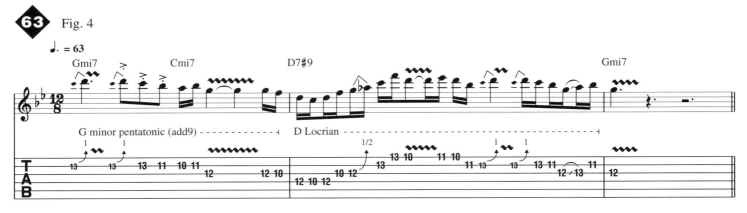

Unlike the other minor modes of the major scale (Dorian, Phrygian, and Aeolian), Locrian does not contain the minor pentatonic scale as its underlying framework. The presence of the ♭5th degree "throws off" the pattern, making it awkward to build upon established licks from that scale. In lieu of the minor pentatonic scale, many players rely on the arpeggiated form of the I chord in Locrian (mi7♭5) as a building block for constructing licks. The following two very useful patterns of the mi7♭5 arpeggio are movable to any key.

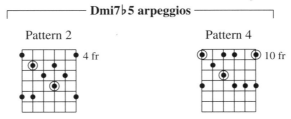

By playing these arpeggios and "sprinkling" in the missing notes (♭2nd, 4th, ♭6th) here and there, the entire Locrian mode is represented. **Fig. 5** gives an example of this process applied to a Dmi7♭5 arpeggio from pattern 2.

64 Fig. 5

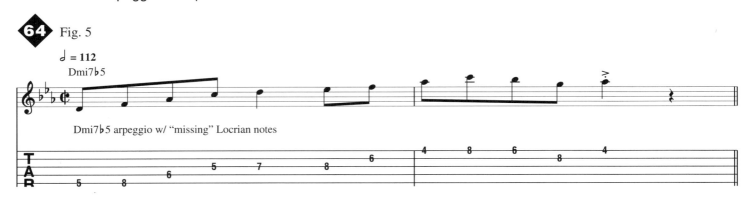

Due to its distinctive quality, the unembellished mi7♭5 arpeggio is often used to "suggest" the Locrian mode. Although the arpeggio omits the ♭2nd, 4th, and ♭6th degrees of the mode, the diminished quality of its triad (root–♭3rd–♭5th) alone is enough to link it to the Locrian mode. **Fig. 6** offers an example with a lick that sequences two patterns (2 and 4) of a Dmi7♭5 arpeggio over a Dmi7♭5 chord. In addition to servicing the Dmi7♭5 chord, the arpeggiated line can be substituted over a B♭9 chord (mi7♭5 arpeggio off the 3rd of a dominant chord).

65 Fig. 6

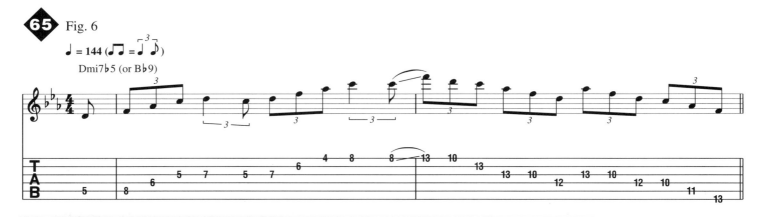

The "ultra-heavy" properties of Locrian make the mode a highly qualified candidate for exploitation in heavy metal music. The combination of the ♭2nd with the "Devil's interval" ♭5th proposes many sinister possibilities for creating ominous sounding riffs. The grinding example in **Fig. 7** uses those two notes (F and B♭) in abundance as it sets the harmonized power chords from the E Locrian mode against a relentless low-E pedal. The inverted E(♭5) chords in the fourth measure are the diatonic power-chord forms of the I chord—in the previous measures only the root is played. While this riff avoids it, many Locrian riffs substitute a standard root/5th power chord for the I chord.

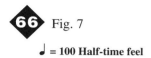

Fig. 7

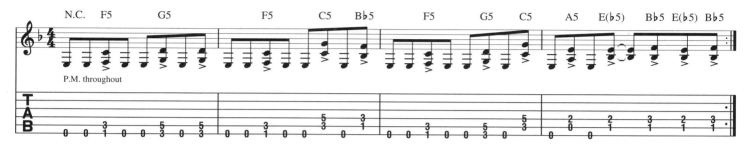

Odds and Ends

Here's a list of additional tips for creating your own Locrian licks. They're all in B Locrian so you can use them in the Play-Along Progression on the CD. When you have them down, transpose them to other keys. Be aware that when applying them, you need to establish the root of Locrian as the pitch axis.

1. Play the B blues scale (B–D–E–F–F♯–A), but *avoid* the 5th (F♯).
2. Play this "synthetic" pentatonic scale: B–C–E–F–A (1–♭2–4–♭5–♭7).
3. Play B°, C, and F major triads. (Combined, they represent every note from B Locrian.)
4. Play an A minor pentatonic scale and add a B.
5. Play a D minor pentatonic scale and add a B.

Play-Along Progression

Use the five patterns of Locrian, located at the top of this chapter, to jam over this B Locrian progression. You can use any of the tips in the "Odds and Ends" section as they are all in B Locrian. Also, try to apply some of the licks in this chapter, changing the rhythms and transposing them where necessary.

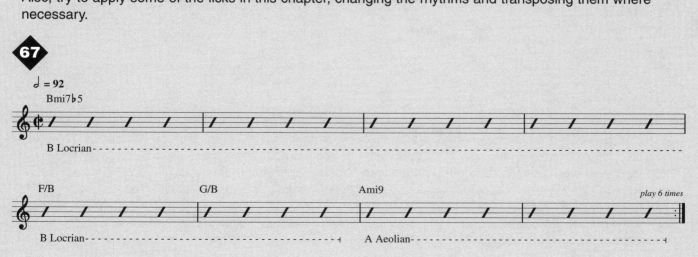

Other Modes

The major scale is *not* unique in containing seven modes. In fact, all diatonic (seven-note) scales have their own set of modes. In this streamlined chapter, we'll take a look at the melodic minor and harmonic minor scales, and the most popular modes from each. Finally, we'll perform a "modal" operation on a nondiatonic scale—the blues scale.

Melodic Minor and Its Modes

The **melodic minor scale** (1–2–♭3–4–5–6–7) can be likened to a major scale with a ♭3rd degree, but it's actually more akin to the Dorian mode with a major 7th. Play through the following three patterns of melodic minor to see if they "feel" familiar to your fingers—like slightly adjusted Dorian patterns. If you make this "connection," you can take your Dorian patterns, raise the ♭7th degrees a half step, or one fret, and you'll have patterns of melodic minor. In like fashion, you can convert your Dorian licks into melodic minor licks by raising the ♭7th degrees by a half step.

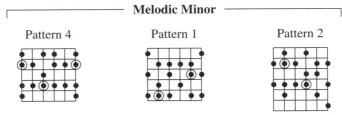

Melodic Minor

Pattern 4   Pattern 1   Pattern 2

Also referred to as "the jazz minor scale," melodic minor can be superimposed over minor triad chords and minor seventh chords for slightly "outside" sounding licks, but it's most commonly used over mi(ma7) chords (root–♭3rd–5th–7th). **Fig. 1** features an Ami(ma7) chord in its usual place, tucked between an Ami chord and an Ami7. A Dorian is used over the Ami chord and segues to A melodic minor, which outlines the tonality change beautifully. Over Ami7, the melody returns to the A Dorian mode.

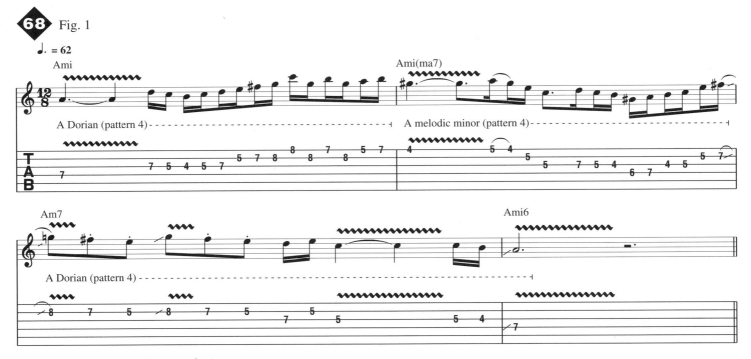

Just as the major scale produces modes built from its seven scale degrees, the same is true of melodic minor. In jazz and fusion, the melodic minor scale and its modes are used extensively for soloing over the colorful chords and daring chord progressions inherent in those styles. We have just seen the "Ionian" mode of the melodic minor scale in action. Now let's take a look at its seventh mode—super-Locrian, or "the altered scale."

The **altered scale** is one of the most popular tools in jazz soloing. Used over functioning (resolving) V chords, it's similar in construction to the Locrian mode. But whereas Locrian contains a perfect 4th, the altered scale has a major 3rd degree. This results in the altered scale containing both a minor and a major 3rd, but most players view its formula as 1–♭9–♯9–3–♭5–♯5–♭7. As you can see, all possible alterations are present: ♭9, ♯9, ♭5, and ♯5. Combined with its major 3rd and ♭7th degrees, this makes the altered scale an ideal choice for soloing over altered dominant chords.

Below are three patterns of the altered scale. Notice they are exactly the same as the melodic minor patterns, except that the 7th degree of melodic minor is now the root (in other words, the altered scale is the seventh mode of melodic minor). This illustrates the popular "shortcut" method for playing an altered scale pattern—go up a half step from the root of a chord and play melodic minor.

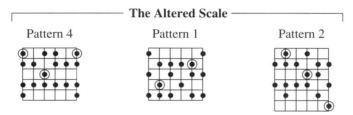

The Altered Scale

Pattern 4   Pattern 1   Pattern 2

Fig. 2 places the G altered scale (seventh mode of A♭ melodic minor) over a G+7♭9 chord which is resolving to Cmi9. Notice that the lick starts on a strong chord tone—the 3rd (B) of G+7♭9—and climbs the scale to hit the root (G) on the downbeat of the next measure, then resolves to the 5th (G) of Cmi9. Targeting strong chord tones on strong beats is imperative in making the altered scale sound musical.

69 Fig. 2

♩ = 138

The sixth mode of melodic minor, **Locrian ♯2**, is constructed just as its name suggests—like the Locrian mode but with a raised 2nd degree: 1–2–♭3–4–♭5–♭6–♭7. Its chief application is over mi7♭5 chords, as an alternative to the Locrian mode. Many players consider the ♭2nd of Locrian too harsh, so they opt for the "softer" sound of Locrian ♯2. As you play through these patterns, try to "feel" the mi7♭5 arpeggios that lie within (see the "Locrian" chapter).

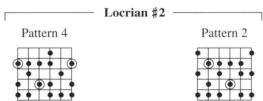

Locrian ♯2

Pattern 4   Pattern 2

Fig. 3 sets the E Locrian ♯2 mode in motion over the II chord (Emi7♭5), and the A altered scale over the V, in a II–V–I progression in D minor. Notice how smoothly the two scales flow into each other.

70 Fig. 3

♩ = 108 (♪♪ = ♪ ♪)

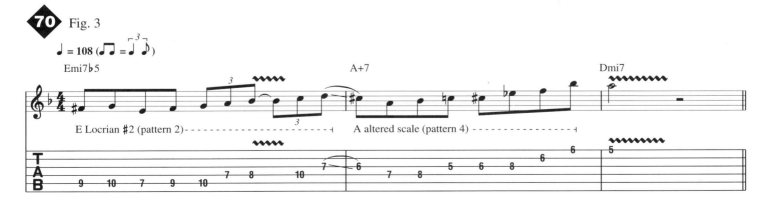

The fourth mode of melodic minor, **Lydian dominant**—or Lydian ♭7—is identical to the Lydian mode of the major scale except that it has, as the name implies, a ♭7th degree: 1–2–3–#4–5–6–♭7. Here are two very practical patterns of Lydian dominant. Play through them slowly, acquainting yourself with the unusual sound of the mode.

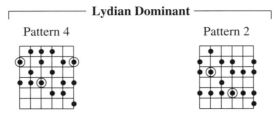

While Lydian dominant and the Lydian mode have much in common in both name and construction, when it comes to application, Lydian dominant is more closely associated with Mixolydian. Like Mixolydian, Lydian dominant is well suited for dominant seventh chords. While its #4th degree puts it especially in line with dominant #11 chords, many guitarists use it over any static or nonresolving dominant chord. **Fig. 4** offers an example of the D Lydian dominant mode over a static D9 chord. The assorted bends, slides, and syncopated rhythms, combined with the notes of the mode itself, make for an interesting mixture of funk, fusion, and blues.

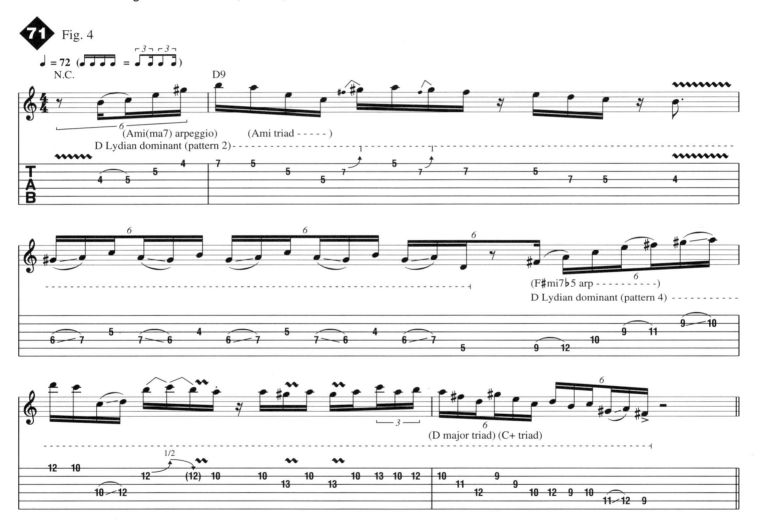

The superimposed arpeggios in the above example—Ami(ma7) and F#mi7♭5 arpeggios; A minor, D major, and C augmented triads—are all harmonized from the parent scale of A melodic minor. As with modes of the major scale, borrowing from the parent scale is quite common among experienced players in dealing with modes of melodic minor. The following chord formulas are harmonized from the key of A melodic minor:

Triads: Ami–Bmi–C+–D–E–F#°–G#°
Seventh chords: Ami(ma7)–Bmi7–Cma7(#5)–D7–E7–F#mi7♭5–G#mi7♭5

Experiment with some of them in arpeggiated form for the following modes: D Lydian dominant, F♯ Locrian ♯2, and the G♯ (or A♭) altered scale. And of course, transpose them to other keys as well.

Fig. 5 serves as a vehicle for stringing the melodic minor scale and three of its modes together all in one progression. It's a II–V–I–IV7 in the key of G minor. The A Locrian ♯2 mode is used for the IImi7♭5 chord (Ami7♭5) and segues to the D altered scale for the V chord (D7♭9). Notice the common tones (D and C) used to tie the two modes together across the bar line. In the third measure, a simple G minor triad drapes the G minor chord followed by selected notes from G melodic minor for the Gmi(ma7). The C Lydian dominant mode is used for the IV7 chord, C9(♯11), and can be seen as a continuation of G melodic minor, as that is its parent scale.

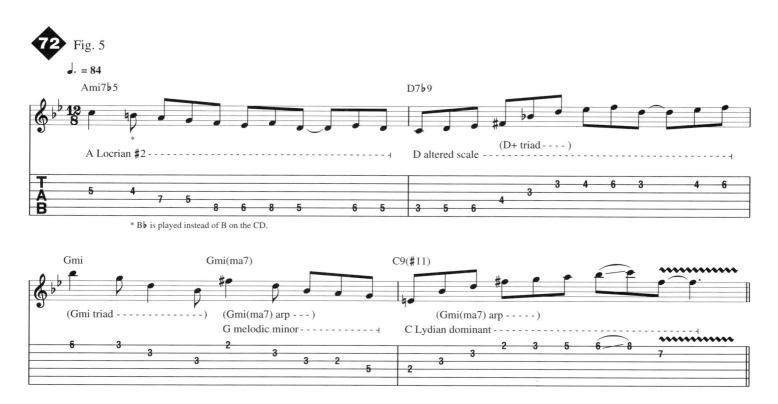

72 Fig. 5

♩. = 84

Ami7♭5   D7♭9

A Locrian ♯2 -| D altered scale -| (D+ triad - - - -)

* B♭ is played instead of B on the CD.

Gmi   Gmi(ma7)   C9(♯11)

(Gmi triad - - - - - - - - - -)   (Gmi(ma7) arp - - -)   (Gmi(ma7) arp - - - - -)
G melodic minor - - - - - - - - - - -| C Lydian dominant -|

Play-Along Progression

This track uses the same progression as Fig. 5. You can use those licks or come up with your own, based on the various patterns you've learned for the melodic minor scale and three of its modes—the altered scale, Locrian ♯2, and Lydian dominant. Start simply, using only a few notes from each mode, and strive to be melodic.

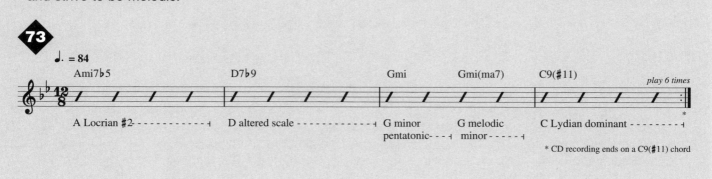

73

♩. = 84

Ami7♭5   D7♭9   Gmi   Gmi(ma7)   C9(♯11)   *play 6 times*

A Locrian ♯2 - - - - - - - - -| D altered scale - - - - - - - - - - -| G minor pentatonic - - -| melodic minor - - - - -| C Lydian dominant - - - - - - -|

* CD recording ends on a C9(♯11) chord

Harmonic Minor and Its Modes

Like melodic minor, the **harmonic minor scale** (1–2–♭3–4–5–♭6–7) has a raised 7th degree. But whereas melodic minor has a "soft" sound due to its natural 6th degree, harmonic minor's ♭6th makes the scale sound more unusual and assertive. This is due chiefly to the minor 3rd "gap" between the ♭6th and 7th degrees, which creates a strong sense of anticipation for resolution—or return to the tonic. Play through these three patterns and listen to the strong "pull" of the scale from its 5th degree to the tonic.

Harmonic Minor

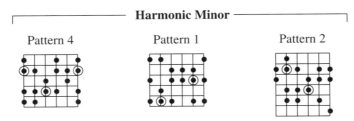

Pattern 4   Pattern 1   Pattern 2

In jazz, harmonic minor is also a popular scale choice for minor-major seventh chords, and it is used in much the same way as melodic minor (see Fig. 1). It is also a favorite among classically-influenced hard rock guitarists such as Yngwie Malmsteen and Tony MacAlpine, and is often used as an alternative to Aeolian. **Fig. 6** offers just such an example with an A harmonic minor run played over an Ami chord.

74 ▶ Fig. 6

Arguably, the most commonly used mode of the harmonic minor scale is **Phrygian dominant**—or the fifth mode. It is constructed like the Phrygian mode of the major scale, except that instead of a minor 3rd degree, it contains a major 3rd (1–♭2–3–4–5–♭6–♭7). Try these three very serviceable patterns.

Phrygian Dominant

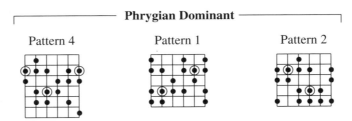

Pattern 4   Pattern 1   Pattern 2

The most common usage of Phrygian dominant is to superimpose it over the functioning V chord in a minor key progression. Jazz, blues, and rock guitarists alike take advantage of the mode's chord-altering capabilities. For example, when the A Phrygian dominant scale (A–B♭–C♯–D–E–F–G) is superimposed over an A7 chord, it outlines the root (A), 3rd (C♯), 5th (E), and ♭7th (G) of the chord, plus the alterations of a ♭9th (B♭) and a ♯5th or ♭13th (F). The D note serves as a "passing" 4th or 11th.

Fig. 7 superimposes the A Phrygian dominant mode over the V chord (A7♭9) in a II–V–I in D minor. This creates tension over the functioning V chord and makes the ear want to hear resolution, which occurs in the D Aeolian melody played over the I chord (Dmi7). (E Locrian is used to outline the Emi7♭5 chord.)

Neoclassical rock guitarists put Phrygian dominant on the rock map in the '80s. Superimposed over power chords, it can be a potent tool when used to fashion sizzling sequences like the one in **Fig. 8**.

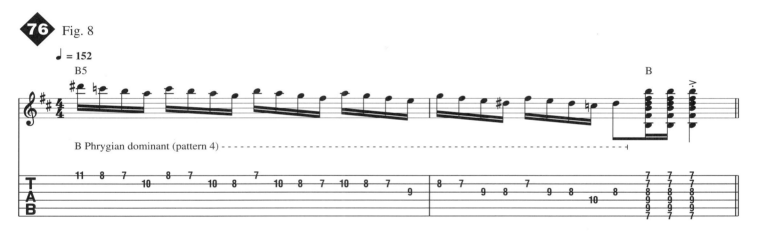

When the harmonic minor scale is harmonized in seventh chords, the resulting formula is Imi(ma7)–IImi7♭5–♭IIIma7♯5–IVmi7–V7–♭VIma7–VII°7. All of these chords can of course be played in arpeggiated form for soloing purposes, but the one that offers the most intriguing possibilities is the VII°7. For example, **Fig. 9** uses the E Phrygian dominant scale over a functioning E7 chord. Any of the arpeggios harmonized from A harmonic minor are up for grabs (A harmonic minor is the parent scale of E Phrygian dominant), but this line only exploits the VII chord, G♯°7. Taking full advantage of the fact that a diminished seventh arpeggio shape repeats itself every three frets, this lick spreads a G♯°7 arpeggio and its inversions (B°7, D°7, and F°7) across the entire second half of this lick.

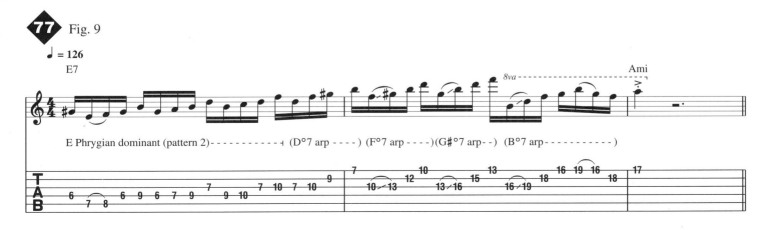

Play-Along Progression

For this Latin rock progression in D minor, play D Aeolian in the first and third measures, and switch to A Phrygian dominant over the V (A7) chords. You might simply want to think "one bar of D Aeolian, one bar of D harmonic minor," etc. Try some G♯°7 arpeggios over the A7 chord as well.

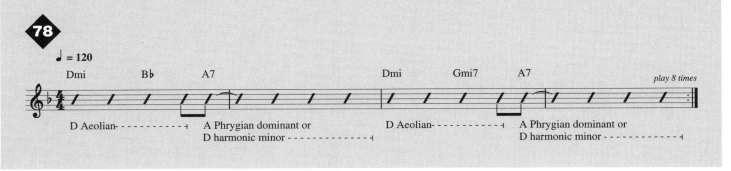

The Blues Scale and Its Modes

The **blues scale** is not a diatonic scale, but that doesn't mean it doesn't contain "modes." Since its construction is unusual to begin with (1–♭3–4–♭5–5–♭7), its modes are equally as unique and are somewhat difficult to apply in the traditional sense. There is one mode of the blues scale, however, that is quite popular, especially among country and country-rock guitarists. Constructed by starting on the ♭3rd degree of the scale, its formula is 1–2–♭3–3–5–6. Known to many as the **"bluegrass scale,"** it's unique in that it holds the basic properties of the major pentatonic scale, while also containing a "bluesy" ♭3rd degree.

Below are two patterns of the blues scale and two patterns of its "second mode"—the bluegrass scale. You will probably notice the resemblance to the relative major/minor pentatonic scale principle—where if you play a minor pentatonic scale pattern starting from the ♭3rd degree you get the relative major pentatonic scale. Some players who use the bluegrass scale think in this relative-major manner and simply transpose their blues-scale licks down a minor 3rd from the root of the chord.

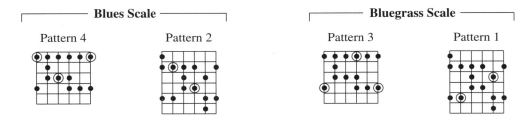

Fig. 10 is an example of the C bluegrass scale in action. Notice the constant mixing of major and minor 3rds, especially in the third measure. Try transposing this lick an octave higher, using pattern 1.

Fig. 11 uses two patterns of the G bluegrass scale in a Southern-rock style solo that utilizes an abundance of finger-slide moves.

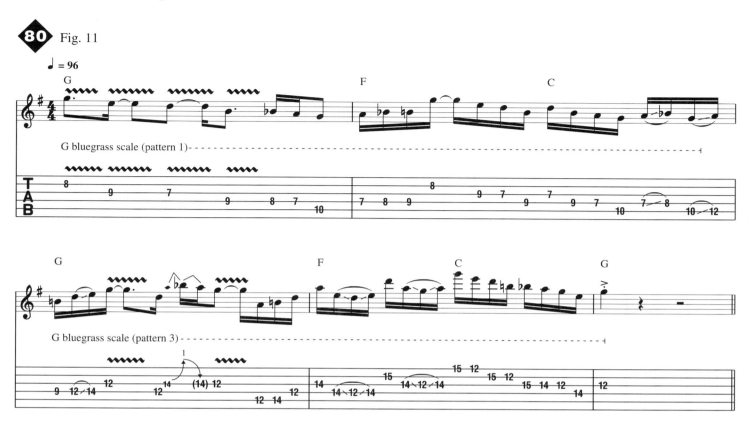

Fig. 11

♩ = 96

Playing the blues scale starting on its 5th degree ("fifth" mode) produces a unique scale (1–♭3–4–♭6–♭7–7) that, with proper care, works well over dominant #9 chords. A good way to apply this mode is to play the blues scale a fourth above (or a fifth below) the root of the chord over which you're soloing. **Fig. 12** gives an example of this process by superimposing A blues scale licks over an E7#9 chord. (When using this method, watch out for the ♭3rd of the pattern you are using—C in this case—as it is the #5th of the chord over which you're playing.)

Fig. 12

♩ = 138

Starting the blues scale on its 4th degree ("third" mode) produces another peculiar scale. Although it contains no 3rd (1–♭2–2–4–5–♭7), by using the ♭2nd degree as a chromatic passing tone, the mode actually works quite well over dominant seventh chords. A good way to experiment with this mode is to play out of a blues scale pattern a fifth above (or a fourth below) the root of the chord. **Fig. 13** offers an example of this method by using notes derived from pattern 4 of the B blues scale to fashion a funky line over an E9.

82 Fig. 13

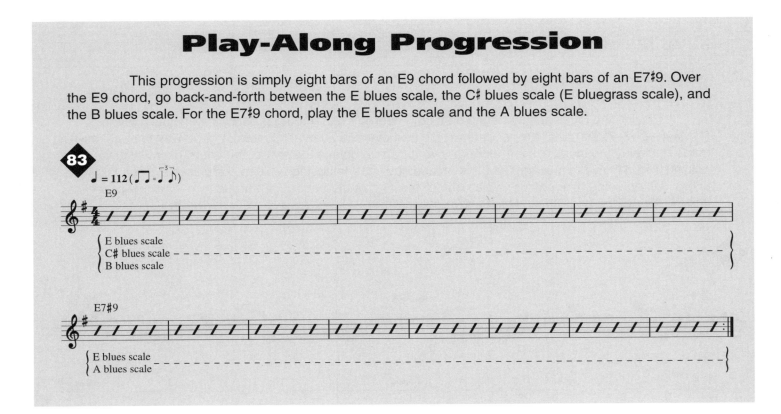

Play-Along Progression

This progression is simply eight bars of an E9 chord followed by eight bars of an E7♯9. Over the E9 chord, go back-and-forth between the E blues scale, the C♯ blues scale (E bluegrass scale), and the B blues scale. For the E7♯9 chord, play the E blues scale and the A blues scale.

Guitar Notation Legend

Guitar Music can be notated three different ways: on a *musical staff*, in *tablature*, and in *rhythm slashes*.

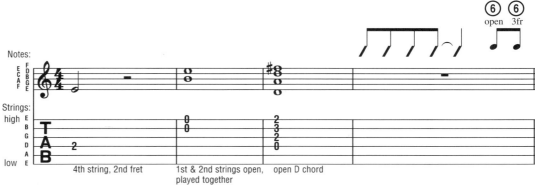

RHYTHM SLASHES are written above the staff. Strum chords in the rhythm indicated. Use the chord diagrams found at the top of the first page of the transcription for the appropriate chord voicings. Round noteheads indicate single notes.

THE MUSICAL STAFF shows pitches and rhythms and is divided by bar lines into measures. Pitches are named after the first seven letters of the alphabet.

TABLATURE graphically represents the guitar fingerboard. Each horizontal line represents a string, and each number represents a fret.

4th string, 2nd fret   1st & 2nd strings open, played together   open D chord

---

HALF-STEP BEND: Strike the note and bend up 1/2 step.

WHOLE-STEP BEND: Strike the note and bend up one step.

GRACE NOTE BEND: Strike the note and immediately bend up as indicated.

SLIGHT (MICROTONE) BEND: Strike the note and bend up 1/4 step.

BEND AND RELEASE: Strike the note and bend up as indicated, then release back to the original note. Only the first note is struck.

PRE-BEND: Bend the note as indicated, then strike it.

VIBRATO: The string is vibrated by rapidly bending and releasing the note with the fretting hand.

WIDE VIBRATO: The pitch is varied to a greater degree by vibrating with the fretting hand.

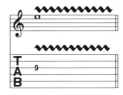

HAMMER-ON: Strike the first (lower) note with one finger, then sound the higher note (on the same string) with another finger by fretting it without picking.

PULL-OFF: Place both fingers on the notes to be sounded. Strike the first note and without picking, pull the finger off to sound the second (lower) note.

LEGATO SLIDE: Strike the first note and then slide the same fret-hand finger up or down to the second note. The second note is not struck.

SHIFT SLIDE: Same as legato slide, except the second note is struck.

TRILL: Very rapidly alternate between the notes indicated by continuously hammering on and pulling off.

TAPPING: Hammer ("tap") the fret indicated with the pick-hand index or middle finger and pull off to the note fretted by the fret hand.

NATURAL HARMONIC: Strike the note while the fret-hand lightly touches the string directly over the fret indicated.

PINCH HARMONIC: The note is fretted normally and a harmonic is produced by adding the edge of the thumb or the tip of the index finger of the pick hand to the normal pick attack.

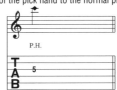

PICK SCRAPE: The edge of the pick is rubbed down (or up) the string, producing a scratchy sound.

MUFFLED STRINGS: A percussive sound is produced by laying the fret hand across the string(s) without depressing, and striking them with the pick hand.

PALM MUTING: The note is partially muted by the pick hand lightly touching the string(s) just before the bridge.

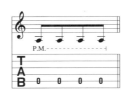

RAKE: Drag the pick across the strings indicated with a single motion.

TREMOLO PICKING: The note is picked as rapidly and continuously as possible.

VIBRATO BAR DIVE AND RETURN: The pitch of the note or chord is dropped a specified number of steps (in rhythm) then returned to the original pitch.

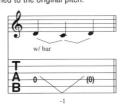

VIBRATO BAR SCOOP: Depress the bar just before striking the note, then quickly release the bar.

VIBRATO BAR DIP: Strike the note and then immediately drop a specified number of steps, then release back to the original pitch.

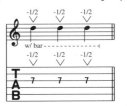

Musicians Institute Press

is the official series of Southern California's renowned music school, Musicians Institute. **MI** instructors, some of the finest musicians in the world, share their vast knowledge and experience with you – no matter what your current level. For guitar, bass, drums, vocals, and keyboards, **MI Press** offers the finest music curriculum for higher learning through a variety of series:

ESSENTIAL CONCEPTS

Designed from MI core curriculum programs.

MASTER CLASS

Designed from MI elective courses.

PRIVATE LESSONS

Tackle a variety of topics "one-on-one" with MI faculty instructors.

BASS

Arpeggios for Bass
by Dave Keif
Private Lessons
00695133 . . . . $12.95

The Art of Walking Bass
A Method for Acoustic or Electric Bass
by Bob Magnusson
Master Class
00695168 Book/CD Pack $17.95

Bass Fretboard Basics
by Paul Farnen
Essential Concepts
00695201 . . . . $12.95

Bass Playing Techniques
by Alexis Sklarevski
Essential Concepts
00695207 . . . . $16.95

Grooves for Electric Bass
by David Keif
Private Lessons
00695265 Book/CD Pack $12.95

Music Reading for Bass
by Wendy Wrehovcsik
Essential Concepts
00695203 . . . . $9.95

Odd-Meter Bassics
by Dino Monoxelos
Private Lessons
00695170 Book/CD Pack $14.95

GUITAR

Advanced Scale Concepts & Licks for Guitar
by Jean Marc Belkadi
Private Lessons
00695298 Book/CD Pack $12.95

Basic Blues Guitar
by Steve Trovato
Private Lessons
00695180 Book/CD Pack $12.95

Contemporary Acoustic Guitar
by Eric Paschal and Steve Trovato
Master Class
00695320 Book/CD Pack $14.95

Creative Chord Shapes
by Jamie Findlay
Private Lessons
00695172 Book/CD Pack $7.95

Diminished Scale for Guitar
by Jean Marc Belkadi
Private Lessons
00695227 Book/CD Pack $9.95

Guitar Basics
by Bruce Buckingham
Private Lessons
00695134 Book/CD Pack $14.95

Guitar Hanon
by Peter Deneff
Private Lessons
00695321 . . . . $9.95

Guitar Soloing
by Dan Gilbert & Beth Marlis
Essential Concepts
00695190 Book/CD Pack $17.95

Harmonics for Guitar
by Jamie Findlay
Private Lessons
00695169 Book/CD Pack $9.95

Jazz Guitar Chord System
by Scott Henderson
Private Lessons
00695291 . . . . $6.95

Jazz Guitar Improvisation
by Sid Jacobs
Master Class
00695128 Book/CD Pack $17.95

Jazz-Rock Triad Improvising
by Jean Marc Belkadi
Private Lessons
00695361 Book/CD Pack $12.95

Modern Approach to Jazz, Rock & Fusion Guitar
by Jean Marc Belkadi
Private Lessons
00695143 Book/CD Pack $12.95

Music Reading for Guitar
by David Oakes
Essential Concepts
00695192 . . . . $16.95

Rhythm Guitar
by Bruce Buckingham & Eric Paschal
Essential Concepts
00695188 . . . . $16.95

Rock Lead Basics
by Nick Nolan & Danny Gill
Master Class
00695144 Book/CD Pack $14.95

Rock Lead Performance
by Nick Nolan & Danny Gill
Master Class
00695278 Book/CD Pack $16.95

Rock Lead Techniques
by Nick Nolan & Danny Gill
Master Class
00695146 Book/CD Pack $14.95

Texas Blues Guitar
by Robert Calva
Private Lessons
00695340 Book/CD Pack $14.95

KEYBOARD

Funk Keyboards –The Complete Method
A Contemporary Guide to Chords, Rhythms, and Licks
by Gail Johnson
Master Class
00695336 Book/CD Pack $14.95

Music Reading for Keyboard
by Larry Steelman
Essential Concepts
00695205 . . . . $12.95

R&B Soul Keyboards
by Henry J. Brewer
Private Lessons
00695327 Book/CD Pack $16.95

Salsa Hanon
by Peter Deneff
Private Lessons
00695226 . . . . $10.95

DRUM

Afro-Cuban Coordination for Drumset
by Maria Martinez
Private Lessons
00695328 Book/CD Pack $14.95

Brazilian Coordination for Drumset
by Maria Martinez
Master Class
00695284 Book/CD Pack $14.95

Chart Reading Workbook for Drummers
by Bobby Gabriele
Private Lessons
00695129 Book/CD Pack $14.95

Drummer's Guide to Odd Meters
by Ed Roscebi
Essential Concepts
00695349 Book/CD Pack $14.95

Working the Inner Clock for Drumset
by Phil Maturano
Private Lessons
00695127 Book/CD Pack $16.95

VOICE

Sightsinging
by Mike Campbell
Essential Concepts
00695195 . . . . $16.95

ALL INSTRUMENTS

An Approach to Jazz Improvisation
by Dave Pozzi
Private Lessons
00695135 Book/CD Pack $17.95

Encyclopedia of Reading Rhythms
by Gary Hess
Private Lessons
00695145 . . . . $19.95

Going Pro
by Kenny Kerner
Private Lessons
00695322 . . . . $22.95

Harmony & Theory
by Keith Wyatt & Carl Schroeder
Essential Concepts
00695161 . . . . $17.95

Lead Sheet Bible
by Robin Randall
Private Lessons
00695130 Book/CD Pack $19.95

WORKSHOP SERIES

Transcribed scores of the greatest songs ever!

Blues Workshop
00695137 . . . . $22.95

Classic Rock Workshop
00695136 . . . . $19.95

FOR MORE INFORMATION, SEE YOUR LOCAL MUSIC DEALER, OR WRITE TO:

HAL•LEONARD®
CORPORATION
7777 W. BLUEMOUND RD. P.O. BOX 13819 MILWAUKEE, WI 53213

Prices, contents, and availability subject to change without notice. Some products may not be available outside of the U.S.A.

0500